Leading the Community College

Leading the Community College

Pathways through an Exponentially Digital Age

Darrel W. Staat

ROWMAN & LITTLEFIELD
Lanham • Boulder • New York • London

Published by Rowman & Littlefield
An imprint of The Rowman & Littlefield Publishing Group, Inc.
4501 Forbes Boulevard, Suite 200, Lanham, Maryland 20706
www.rowman.com

86-90 Paul Street, London EC2A 4NE, United Kingdom

Copyright © 2022 by Darrel W. Staat

All rights reserved. No part of this book may be reproduced in any form or by any electronic or mechanical means, including information storage and retrieval systems, without written permission from the publisher, except by a reviewer who may quote passages in a review.

British Library Cataloguing in Publication Information Available

Library of Congress Cataloging-in-Publication Data
Name: Staat, Darrel W., 1941–, author.
Title: Leading the community college : pathways through an exponentially digital age / Darrel W. Staat.
Description: Lanham : Rowman & Littlefield, 2022. | Includes bibliographical references. | Summary: "Leading the Community College: Pathways Through an Exponentially Digital Age provides information about ten twenty-first century technologies, their probable impact on community colleges, and guidance to community college presidents as to how to successfully deal with the technologies as they move from the linear stage to the exponential stage"—Provided by publisher.
Identifiers: LCCN 2021059334 (print) | LCCN 2021059335 (ebook) | ISBN 9781475865295 (cloth) | ISBN 9781475865301 (paperback) | ISBN 9781475865318 (epub)
Subjects: LCSH: Community colleges—Administration. | Educational leadership. | Educational technology. | Education, Higher—Effect of technological innovations on.
Classification: LCC LB2328 .S72 2022 (print) | LCC LB2328 (ebook) | DDC 378.1/543—dc23/eng/20211231
LC record available at https://lccn.loc.gov/2021059334
LC ebook record available at https://lccn.loc.gov/2021059335

Contents

Preface		vii
Acknowledgments		xiii
Introduction		xv
1	Two Centuries	1
2	Envisioning the Future	13
3	Business in an Exponential Age	21
4	Seven Technologies	33
5	The Big Three Technologies	47
6	Revisions	59
7	Securing the Future	69
8	Students	75
9	Learning Methods	83
10	Pathways	95
11	Commingling with Business	107
12	Eye to the Future	113

Epilogue	119
Appendix: Guiding the Community College: A Two-Phase System	121
References	123
About the Author	125

Preface

Although my experience spans more than forty years of community college teaching and administration and another seven years as a university faculty member teaching graduate students interested in becoming higher education administrators, I started my working career as an electrician. When I was twelve years old, my father, who was an electrician, took me with him to a house he was going to wire. At the time, I knew nothing about what he was doing. At the house, which was under construction, there were studs that outlined the rooms inside and little more.

THE BLUEPRINT

He unwrapped a blueprint and explained how it was actually a picture of the house's floor plan. He told me that we would place boxes on the walls and ceilings that were indicated on the blueprint; they indicated where the receptacles and lights would be installed. We walked around the house, and he marked on the studs where the boxes for receptacles and light switches would be placed.

LEARNING THE PROCESS

He showed me that there were lines on the sides of the metal boxes and explained that when a box was placed on the stud, it should stick out a bit, aligning the line on the outside of the box with the edge of the stud. When I learned that process to meet his satisfaction, he told me to go into each room and nail the receptacle boxes in place. Next, he demonstrated how to drill holes in the center of the studs about two feet above the floor. He told me to drill the holes in each stud between the boxes. When I finished drilling the holes, he showed me how to remove wire from the box it came in.

He explained that the wires, when installed, created a circuit. I asked what a circuit was. He said to think about it as water going through a hose to each of the boxes, which were like sprinklers; the power in the wires came from the breaker box, which was like a hose bib on the outside of a house. Over a period of time, he explained how to install the breaker box and run wires to the breaker box for each circuit, which was connected to the service box on the outside of the house.

To finish the house for occupancy, we would return later and install the receptacles, switches, light fixtures, and breakers themselves. When it was all hooked up, we checked every receptacle and light to see if it worked properly. Nine years after that first day with him, I took the journeyman's exam and passed it with flying colors.

TRANSFER OF LEARNING

What did I learn wiring a house that had anything to do with becoming a successful community college president? To begin with I learned to enjoy working with carpenters, HVAC technicians, plumbers, brick layers, roofers, painters, and all the kinds of workers who make home building construction a reality in America. I learned to appreciate their work ethics, their humor, and their ability to complete a fairly complicated task efficiently. I appreciated their attitude of getting the job done appropriately, regardless of the obstacles they faced from one job to the next. I found that faculty in the technical programs in a community college were very similar to those I had worked with in the house construction business. I understood them and appreciated what they could do.

I learned how to picture a completed house from looking at a blueprint. I learned to see the big picture. Finally, I learned to get to work on time, stick with the job until it was finished, and take pride in what my part in the work entailed. To me, leading a community college took the same kind of basic skills: get to work on time; plan out the day, week, month, and year; always be looking ahead; complete what was begun in a timely manner within budget; and always do the job in the ethical manner. As it turned out, learning how to wire a house was a solid foundation for a successful career in higher education.

LEAVING THE ELECTRICAL TRADE

When I graduated from college with a BA in English, I left the electrical trade to become a public school teacher. Within three years, while teaching, I completed an MA in English and accepted a teaching job in a community college. After four years teaching at a community college, I enrolled in a doctoral program. Two years later, I graduated with a doctorate in English. That led to a teaching position in another community college, which prepared me to be promoted to the position of dean and the beginning of a successful administrative career.

ADMINISTRATIVE EXPERIENCE

That being said, this book is an attempt to guide those in community college leadership how to be successful in their careers over the next few decades. This book will reflect my experience in teaching and administration, which led to a second career at the university level teaching graduate students, and the need for research, writing, and publication. My teaching, working as a coordinator of a doctoral program, plus research, writing, and publishing led to another kind of journeyman level—that of associate professor.

WORK OF THE PRESIDENT

I found that successfully leading a community college in the twentieth century as president took a great deal of time and effort guiding growth, funding shortfalls, planning for the future, raising alternative funds, resolving personnel issues, planning for recruitment and retention of students, supporting faculty and staff development, working with the college board, constructing new facilities, renovating existing facilities, developing off-campus centers and campuses, working with elected officials, supporting training needs of business and industry, and the list goes on. There was always too much to do and never enough time or funding to support everything that could be done.

TWENTY-FIRST-CENTURY OPPORTUNITIES

By the time the twenty-first century arrived, community college presidents soon learned that there were more opportunities, more technologies to deal with, and less funding to support their efforts to keep the community colleges moving ahead. While none of the twentieth-century segments of the job disappeared and some became more complicated, the president, staff and faculty, students, and the community were faced with ten technologies that were developing rapidly that would disrupt the business and educational landscape without asking permission, and often without the knowledge of those leading and working within the community college.

LEARNING ON THE JOB

For community college leaders, the first twenty years of the new century was a time to scramble to keep up for some, and for others, a time to look in disbelief as to what was going on and what was promised for the future. By 2021, the impact of ten technologies was rapidly moving toward fruition, not decades away anymore, but just years. It was like standing on the deck of a mid-nineteenth-century sailing vessel heading directly toward a storm on all sides or, better described, toward a hurricane of tremendous width. Although the ship was sailing along pretty much under control at the moment, it was clear to see that disruptions were not far away.

PURPOSE OF THIS BOOK

The purpose of this book to is to assist twenty-first century presidents and leaders in community colleges to not only understand what is facing their institutions in terms of disruption by ten technologies, but how to go about dealing with each of them successfully. The pathway for success in the twenty-first century comes from considerable research into the issues facing community college leaders. The research provides a compass reading or stars that guide the way toward an accurate understanding of the situations to be faced, and appropriate actions taken to work with them. Being prepared is important; taking the best actions are critical to success.

Overall, although community colleges may make significant changes in how they operate in the future, the long-range goal is to keep the institutions in place to serve the needs of students, faculty, staff, the business community, local economic development, and the constituents who live and work within the service area of the college. It is important to keep moving ahead successfully. It is wise to remember that "The college that isn't going forward is going backward" (Fisher, 1984).

Acknowledgments

I would like to thank the many graduate students at Wingate University who inspire me beyond teaching, to research and write. This book is for each of them who will venture seriously into community college and university leadership.

I greatly appreciate the encouragement and support of Dr. Charlesa Hann, assistant dean of Wingate University's School of Education.

I cannot say enough in my appreciation for my colleague Dr. John McKay at Wingate University. He inspires me to keep on going.

As always, my thanks to my wife, Beverly, who has learned to live with someone who incessantly buys books, works for hours at a time in his office, and writes books. She is a gem.

Introduction

The community college president in the twenty-first century is heading into unknown territory equipped with ideas and concepts that were successful in the past. Before him or her lies an unprecedented new environment. On one hand, what appears to be the same are students, faculty, staff, the business community, local economic development, and elected officials. The president still has to deal with them all. On the other hand is a set of ten technologies that will cause disruptions in what must be taught to students, how students should be taught, what the job market looks like, how faculty will need to adapt to new teaching methods, and what the business community will demand from graduates.

This book will review the differences in leading a community college in the twentieth and the twenty-first centuries. What made good sense to William Rainey Harper, the founding president of the University of Chicago who designed the junior college, will differ significantly from what those leading community colleges will face in the next decade and beyond. This book explains the differences between linear and exponential thinking, an understanding needed by twenty-first century leaders. All ten technologies currently under development have the potential to move onto the scene with the speed of Amazon, Uber, and Airbnb. An understanding of what is coming and how to successfully deal with it is critical to success in the near future.

Visionary thinking must become commonplace. Successful business leaders will be required to become futurists and visionaries in order to stay in business (Johnson & Suskewicz, 2020). Many leaders in the business community are already aware of the changes they face and are taking action to prepare for and adapt to them. They have no choice. If businesses are to stay viable, they have to modify their approaches and actions for success. If they do not, their competitors will. Although the business community in general is working hard to stay abreast of the disruptions the ten technologies will bring, it seems that many community college leaders are ignoring the coming changes, or are at best making small modifications to deal with them.

It seems clear from research that successful community college leaders, similar to business executives in this century, will need to reconstruct their institutions. Program offerings will change, faculty will need to be upgraded, students will need to learn in new ways, and the business community will continually require new skill training. There may even be some extensive changes, like merging community colleges with businesses. Community college leaders must understand what the leader of Amazon stated, that it is important to "focus on the long term. It's all about the long term" (Bezos, 2021, p. 21).

How are community colleges secured for the future? It will take continual learning, in-depth understanding, and appropriate actions based on solid research to determine what makes a community college successful in the twenty-first century. The goal of this book is to provide clues to the pathways to success. The community college movement must continue to serve the learning needs of students, the training needs of the business community, and the collaborative directional needs of local economic development. Even though the methods will change due to the disruptions of the ten technologies, the mission being adapted to those changes must continue for the benefit of all concerned.

Chapter 1

Two Centuries

What a difference a century makes. In the late nineteenth century, William Rainey Harper, founding president of the University of Chicago, developed a two-year educational program within the university to serve students in their preparation for the work needed to complete the bachelor's degree. Over the years, his initial idea went through several iterations to become the junior college, which grew and flourished in the early twentieth century. It served those who had graduated high school and were interested in higher education, but for whom there literally was not enough room in the existing colleges and universities.

THE JUNIOR COLLEGE

By the 1920s, Harper's idea had become a set of independent two-year colleges which served students interested in transferring to a four-year university to obtain a bachelor's degree. Although that pathway in the junior colleges worked well, in addition, since the schools were independent and placed in various cities and across the country, they soon began to offer programs that prepared graduates to work in business and industry. Harper's idea of setting up a junior college within a university morphed into a set of two-year colleges that went far beyond his initial thinking.

The junior college developed like wildfire across the country in many states. It seemed that the individuals who graduated from high schools and wanted a higher education saw the junior college as a first critical step in preparing them for an academic career or job in the ever-expanding business world. By the 1960s, the junior college became what is known today as the community college, serving transfer students, and a wide spectrum of workforce needs including health, technical, business, computers, and most anything else in the business world that needed training.

COMMUNITY COLLEGES

To keep the junior college viable over the years, it took leadership that helped the junior colleges adapt to an ever-changing environment including, the Great Depression in the 1930s, World War II in the 1940s, the Cold War of the 1950s, and the growing need for more education and training. It culminated in the 1960s with the arrival of the community college, which served students interested in transferring to a four-year college or university or those who wanted preparation for entry into the expanding numbers of jobs in the fields of health, technical programs, business, computers, and the like. What the students wanted, what the business community needed, and what the economic development foresaw, became the domain of the community college.

ADAPTABLE LEADERSHIP

That notion of adaptable leadership was underscored by Edward Morrison, who wrote, "The adaptive leader develops the skill of asking clear, adaptive questions. Being an adaptive leader requires that you be open to experimentation and innovation in or to generate answers to your adaptive questions" (Morrison et al., 2019, p.43). The Great Depression did not slow the development of junior colleges, rather students flocked to the institutions for training and education that would lead to jobs.

When training for the military was needed for the war effort, the junior colleges stepped up and did their part. During World War II, those leading junior colleges found themselves developing programs for the war effort including navigation, aviation training, airplane instrumentation, photography, surveying, and riveting. Following the war, junior colleges played a critical role in educating and training the war veterans who used the GI bill. During the late 1950s, the enrollment stalled and fell off a bit, but not for long.

THE 1960S

With the arrival of the baby boomers, which provided a tremendous increase in student numbers, the 1960s saw community colleges develop and expand in every state in the union. There seemed to be no end for the need for institutions of higher education that served a wide variety of needs. It took serious leadership and hard work to adapt to the expansion of numbers of high school graduates who were interested in pursuing associate and bachelor's degrees, business and health training needs, and technical technician needs.

Community colleges rapidly replaced junior colleges during the decade. New community colleges were being developed at an accelerated rate, so much so that finding administrators and faculty was difficult. Many were drawn from the public schools. At the same time, state funding for the community college had a hard time keeping up with the needs, which led to significant amounts of adjunct faculty being hired, a trait that has never lessened to the present day.

Later, as community colleges came into their own, George Vaughan stated, "Since its inception, the fundamental qualities of the community college have been responsiveness and flexibility in meeting the education needs of our society" (Vaughan, 1983, p. 232). Community college leaders over the decades learned the importance of serving the needs of the local community, understood that an entrepreneurial approach was necessary, and developed institutions that served the needs of students and the work forces they would join.

TWENTIETH-CENTURY COMMUNITY COLLEGE LEADERSHIP

Successful community college leadership in the twentieth century required a mindset of moving ahead at all times. As one decade moved to the next, community college presidents had to modify their ideas, understandings, and actions to meet the needs that arose. Many learned how to do that very well and led colleges that were highly successful. The twentieth-century model they followed and creatively modified over the years worked well for students, faculty, staff, the business community and local economic development. It was relatively easy to see what needed to be done, and adaptation was the reasonable path that led to success for all concerned.

THE NEW CENTURY

When the twenty-first century arrived, everything appeared pretty much the same. The cross-over to the new century did not create an information technology (IT) disaster as many pundits predicted. For the most part, IT provided a smooth ride into the new century. In addition, there was the Internet, which seemed to be quite helpful, and email which really did speed communication up considerably. There was an internet-driven bookstore; there were Blackberrys in pants pockets or carried on belts of millions of people, and there was a great deal of excitement about what the internet would bring. Other than that, life seemed to go on as normal; community college leaders led their institutions pretty much as they had in the twentieth century.

2007

The wake-up call came in 2007, when the digital world suddenly took a number of steps forward. Most likely that year will be looked upon by historians in the future as a significant turning point. For many, most likely 2007 will be remembered as the year the country began the rapid slide into the Great Recession. Banks, that had made home loans much too easy led the downfall. Businesses large and small took a real beating. Congress had to take unprecedented steps financially to help businesses and financial institutions stay afloat. All that and more happened, but that is not the reason 2007 is a very special historical year. The reason is that a number of digital things happened near to and in 2007.

- In late 2006, Google brought YouTube on the scene.
- In 2007, Steve Jobs announced the iPhone.

- Storage capacity exploded, thanks to Hadoop, which made the cloud possible.
- Twitter appeared.
- Amazon released Kindle.
- IBM introduced Watson, the computer that beat the two best players of *Jeopardy*.
- Intel, the world's largest chip maker, created a new IT building block that paved the way for much faster processors.
- Uber and Air Bed and Breakfast were envisioned.

Reactions to 2007

Where were most Americans in 2007? Working at their jobs and living their lives, wondering what the iPhone thing was. What was wrong with flip phones? They were so cool; they made *Star Trek* seem so close. Who was ever going to bother using Twitter? Why read a book on a computer when printed books did the job so well? The Watson computer beat the two best *Jeopardy* players in the world, so what?

Those things were all there; it seemed like they appeared suddenly, but not too much notice taken. Community colleges went on as usual and, in most cases, increasing in numbers significantly while experiencing severe reductions in state funding as a result of the Great Recession. Community college leadership found itself in a quandary and took drastic measures in many cases to stay alive and viable. It was also a time when some presidents threw in the towel and retired. Others found ways to keep their institutions moving ahead despite problems on all sides.

Leadership in the Twenty-First Century

Moving ahead toward the third decade of the twenty-first century, there are massive changes on all sides. Today, the world is heading in directions that until recently were science fiction, maybe fun for the movie goer, but of no serious consequence. However, the world is changing phenomenally, rapidly, and for better or worse, depending on what is experienced and most importantly, what is understood. Community college leaders need to know as much as possible about the technology world that is coming at them rapidly on multiple fronts in order to lead their colleges successfully.

TEN TECHNOLOGIES

What is it that is coming at breakneck speed? Ten twenty-first century technologies are autonomous vehicles, 3D printing, the internet of things, medical genome development, agricultural genome development, personal robots, bitcoin/blockchain, quantum computing, artificial intelligence, and nanotechnology. Those ten technologies, plus combinations of many of them, may actually double that number. Some of them will be relatively reasonable to deal with and others will be extremely difficult. Some will make important improvements in lives of Americans and people throughout the world; while others have the potential to cause serious disruptions in societies and cultures across the planet.

These ten twenty-first technologies will impact community colleges because they develop in a very different way than inventions developed in the twentieth century. Take the development of the automobile in the twentieth century, for instance; it began with a gasoline engine connected to what had been a horse-drawn carriage. It took about thirty years for an all-steel car body to be built with the engine in the front. Ford's Model A is good example of that kind of car. Cars developed slowly over the decades, and it took about one hundred and thirty years to reach the modern automobile. It took until the mid-1960s for the Ford Mustang to appear.

The Impact of the Transistor

In the late 1950s, scientists were able to place a transistor on a chip about the size of a thumbnail. That seemingly small success meant that it would not take long before vacuum tubes would be replaced by silicon chips, or what became known as solid state. Engineers soon figured how to put two transistors on a chip, then four, pretty soon eight, after a while sixteen, and so on. In 1965, Gordon Moore observed that, given the rapidly increasing number of transistors per chip, computer power seemed to be doubling every year. A little later, he revised that to a doubling every two years, but as time went by, Moore's Law came to mean that the number of transistors on a chip was actually doubling about every eighteen months.

Growth of Transistors

That doubling of transistors on a chip, and the computer power and storage it generates in eighteen months, is still true today. In 1957, there was the first transistor placed on a chip. Over the years the doubling process, known as Moore's Law, has increased the number of transistors on a chip in 2021 to 2.6 trillion.

Penny Doubling

The explanation of this seemingly unbelievable increase has to do with the doubling of the number of transistors on a chip in every eighteen months. To help to understand this situation is the penny-doubling scenario. Given the choice to receive $100,000 per day for a one-month period of thirty days or receive one penny on the first day, which would double every day for thirty days, what would obtain the best outcome? In thirty days, the $100,000 per day accumulates to $3.0 million. On the other hand, doubling a penny every day for thirty days would add up to $5.3 million. Continue the process for two more days and the $100,000 per day becomes $3.2 million, while the penny-doubling becomes $21.2 million.

Linear and Exponential Growth

This comparison clearly demonstrates the difference between a linear growth process and an exponential growth process. A linear growth process increases similar to the $100,000 a day process. It is like most things experienced in life, one day follows another, a child grows up year by year, and change happens in at a predictable, reasonable rate that everyone is used to. Exponential development, on the other hand, is something different altogether. It develops like the penny-doubling example.

At first the item develops at a predictable linear rate. It grows gradually from day-to-day until it reaches a certain point, in the example of the month, about day twenty-six. Then suddenly it increases at an astronomical rate. Earlier in this chapter were listed the ten technologies. Up until now, all of those technologies, with the exception of quantum computing, have been affected by Moore's Law. The technologies develop in two stages. In stage one, they develop in a linear growth manner. In stage two, they develop in an exponential growth manner. Quantum Computing is in a class by itself, developing velocity far beyond a stage two exponential stage.

Two-Stage Process

Nine of the ten technologies cited above are developing in this two-stage process. In stage one, the linear stage, they seem to be developing in a normal, predictable fashion. However, when they reach a certain point, they move to stage two and take off like a rocket. It is exponential development that makes them accelerate so fast. Nine of the ten of the technologies cited above are still in stage one at the moment. The reason a person may not be aware of some of them is because they are developing in stage one, like most everything else observed in the world. However, stage two is on the way soon.

Uber, Airbnb, and Amazon

There are obvious examples of where the exponential stage two came into play, such as Uber, Airbnb, and Amazon. One year the Uber and Airbnb were interesting ideas, seemingly crazy brainstorms. However, when Uber hit the exponential stage two, within a very few years, it became the largest people transportation system in the world, outnumbering all the taxis in the world. The same process took place with Airbnb. When Airbnb reached stage two, it suddenly became the largest room service organization in the world. Both Uber and Airbnb were able to grow so fast because of computer power and cloud storage that had already grown exponentially, thanks to Moore's law.

Amazon developed in much the same way. It started as an online bookstore that gave consumers access to more books in one source than any standard brick and mortar bookstore could ever hope to offer. When Jeff Bezos found how well the online bookstore process worked, he soon expanded to other products and within a matter of a few years, Amazon was outcompeting not only bookstores, but other retail organizations, which had been in operation for decades or more (Bezos, 2021). Uber, Airbnb, and Amazon all took advantage of vastly increased computer power, algorithms, and computer storage, which had developed along the lines of Moore's law.

Impact of the Ten Technologies

Chapters 4 and 5 will discuss the impact of the ten technologies, and what actions must be taken to deal with them. Each of the ten technologies will to some degree disrupt the business community, the health community, the military community, and community colleges. What has been business as usual will become business in a different way. While seven of the technologies will create serious impacts, the other three have the potential to wreak havoc. Those in leadership positions, including community college presidents, administrators, faculty, and staff will have to be well informed as to which technologies are developing in stage one, how rapidly they will move to stage two, and what actions to take in order to deal with them successfully.

CONCLUSION

Change created by the ten technologies, if not prepared for, will seem to appear from nowhere and develop with astronomical acceleration. It is clear to see, community college leadership in the twenty-first century will need to be of a different ilk from that in the past century in order to keep the institutions operating successfully for all concerned. This book will make every effort to assist and support those in leadership to be able to handle the technologies for the benefit of students, faculty, staff, board members, the business community, and local economic development. Successful community college leadership will take serious time and effort on the part of the leadership. It will not be for the faint of heart.

CHAPTER 1 SUMMARY

- In the late nineteenth century, William Rainey Harper, president of the University of Chicago, developed a two-year educational program at the university to serve as preparation for the work needed to complete the bachelor's degree at the University of Chicago.
- By the 1920s, Harper's idea had become a set of independent two-year colleges that served students interested in transferring to a four-year university to obtain a bachelor's degree.

- In the long run, the junior college developed like wildfire across the country in several states.
- It culminated in the 1960s with the arrival of the community college.
- The Great Depression did not slow the development of junior colleges; rather, students flocked to the institutions for training and education that would lead to jobs.
- During World War II, leading junior colleges found themselves developing programs for the war effort including navigation, aviation training, airplane instrumentation, photography, surveying, and riveting.
- The 1960s saw tremendous economic growth and the arrival of the baby boomers interested in higher education.
- State funding for the community college had a hard time keeping up with the needs, which led to significant amounts of adjunct faculty being hired, a trait that never left up to the present day.
- As can be seen, the junior college movement attracted leaders that had to be entrepreneurial to meet the needs created by the community college movement.
- Successful community college leadership in the twentieth century required a mindset of moving ahead at all times.
- The crossover to the new century did not create an IT disaster as many pundits were concerned about and predicted.
- The wakeup call came in 2007, when the digital world suddenly came alive.
- The reason is that a number of digital things happened near to and in 2007.
- In late 2006, Google brought YouTube on the scene.
- In 2007, Steve Jobs announced the iPhone.
- Storage capacity exploded, thanks to Hadoop, which made the cloud possible.
- Twitter appeared.
- Amazon released Kindle.
- IBM introduced Watson, the computer that beat the two best players of *Jeopardy*.
- Intel, the world's largest chip maker, created a new IT building block that paved the way for much faster processors.
- Uber and Airbnb were envisioned.

- Community colleges went on as usual and, in most cases, increasing in numbers significantly while experiencing severe reductions in state funding.
- Moving ahead to the third decade of the twenty-first century, there are massive changes on all sides.
- Community college leaders need to know as much as possible about the world that is coming at them rapidly on multiple fronts to lead their colleges successfully.
- These ten twenty-first technologies will impact community colleges, and the world for that matter, because they develop in a very different way than inventions developed in the twentieth century.
- Cars developed slowly over the decades and it took over one hundred and thirty years to get to the modern automobile.
- In the late 1950s, scientists were able to place a transistor on a chip about the size of a thumbnail.
- Moore's Law came to mean that the number of transistors on a chip was actually doubling about every eighteen months.
- That doubling of transistors on a chip and the computer power and storage it generates in eighteen months is still true today.
- Transistors on a chip have gone from one in 1957 to 2.6 trillion in 2021.
- An example to help to understand this situation is penny-doubling.
- The penny-doubling comparison clearly demonstrates the difference between a linear growth process and an exponential growth process.
- The technologies develop in two stages. In stage one, they develop in a linear growth manner. In stage two, they develop in an exponential growth manner.
- All ten of the technologies cited above are still in stage one at the moment.
- There are obvious examples of where the exponential stage two came into play, such as Uber, Airbnb, and Amazon.
- Both Uber and Airbnb were able to grow so fast because of computer power and cloud storage that had already grown exponentially, thanks to Moore's law.
- Uber, Airbnb, and Amazon all took advantage of vastly increased computer power, algorithms, and computer storage which had developed because of Moore's law.

- Seven of the technologies will create serious impacts, and the other three have to potential to wreak havoc.
- This book will make every effort to assist and support those in leadership to be able to handle the technologies for the benefit of students, faculty, staff, board members, the business community, and local economic development.

Chapter 2

Envisioning the Future

"Unless the president articulates a special vision, mission, or cause for the institution, he or she will not be viewed as a true leader."—Fisher, 1984, p. 57

Although James Fisher wrote the above statement in the mid-1980s, it remains true today. In addition, looking forward into the next twenty years, true leaders will be required to keep community colleges intact and viable in a period of rapid, accelerating change. The future will demand a "special vision, mission and cause," if the leadership expects to guide the institution successfully through the potential disruptions made by the ten technologies.

TWENTY-FIRST-CENTURY ISSUES

In general, the issues facing the community college during the next two decades will stretch the current skills and abilities of presidents, college administration, faculty, and staff tremendously. They will have to have become aware of what is on the horizon, alert all constituents of the college about what is heading toward the institution, and create plans to deal with each of the technologies that will impact their colleges. If they are unaware of what is coming, have not communicated directly with the faculty, staff, students, board members, and local business leaders, and have not made plans for the disruptions, they will find themselves in a perilous situation.

Chapters 4 and 5 will discuss the ten technologies which exist in the twenty-first century that will have direct impact on community college across the country with disruptions that will affect courses taught, programs offered, programs modified, teaching methods changed, faculty members upgraded, staff trained, equipment and facilities added, service to the community the college served, and most importantly, the students enrolled in the institution. It will become obvious to all that the twenty-first century is developing very differently than the twentieth. Preparing for changes on all fronts will face community college leaders.

"Preparing for a challenging future requires that you allow yourself to be open to options you may have rejected in the past or to approaches you find uncomfortable at first" (Willyerd and Mistick, 2016, p. 65). It will be critical on the part of community college leaders and faculty to be willing to investigate the future possibilities in order to understand the disruptions that will affect the institution, the faculty, teaching methods, the staff, students, and the business community. Changes will be needed in terms of what is to be taught, how it should be learned, and how the instruction supports the rapidly changing business community.

PREPARING FOR THE FUTURE

What does a community college president do to prepare for the future? In simplest terms, he or she must use visionary thinking to the maximum. What is happening today or this week obviously needs attention, but what may happen in the future also needs high priority. The presidents and other leaders in the community college must become future-focused. That is to say, they must understand what kind of disruptions the technologies may create; research the potential time frame for the disruptions; discuss the future possibilities with faculty, staff, board members, and local business leaders; make plans; and take appropriate action.

LEADING BACK FROM THE FUTURE

It will be very useful to lead in a different way, one described as back from the future (Johnson and Suskewicz, 2020). The process begins with the development of a vision describing what the college will be facing twenty years out. This vision must come from serious, continuous research into the development of each of the ten technologies. As the technologies reach stage two, exponential, they will have direct impacts on the college in terms of courses to be taught, programs to be developed, faculty development needed, teaching and learning methods needed for the students, training for the staff, clarification for the board members, and media information for those in the service area of the college.

It is important to envision the college twenty years out, understand what the possibilities are, and then plan back to the present. This will allow the college to create strategic plans that determine the equipment needed, faculty training and education that is necessary, and the renovation of existing facilities, or construction of additional facilities. Further, it will allow the president time to plan the financial needs of the institution, work with the members of the general assembly for data-driven funding, discover grant possibilities, and develop capital campaigns, which together will allow the college to meet the financial needs for both the present and the future.

FUTURE BACK VS. PRESENT FORWARD PLANNING

There is a big difference between planning from the future back to the present, and planning forward from the present to the future. When planning from the present to the future, the president and the college will be entangled in what is happening in the present. That kind of planning may have worked well in the twentieth century, but will only put the college in a position in which it is unable to successfully deal with rapid, accelerating changes in the future. Rather, the president and those in leadership positions in the college must stretch their thinking supported with appropriate, in-depth research out to a point of twenty years into the future.

FUTURE BACK VISIONING

That kind of visioning will allow the president and leaders in the college prepare for what is coming. The expectations should be for a world very different from the present. If the research is carefully developed with the greatest possible accuracy, then a reasonable vision of a future twenty years out can be designed. Using that vision, the school can then develop a dynamic, strategic planning process leading toward that vision. Even then, the plans will need to be open-ended to allow for change as new research information is discovered.

That is not to say that whatever is researched will become the actual situation in the future, but that the leadership has seriously investigated what could become future reality. The planning may have to be modified as time goes by, but the leadership will have a foundation from which to work from in making sound decisions. Since the college does much to serve the training needs of business and industry, it is imperative that the college develops in parallel with the successful business community. Otherwise, the college will find itself unable to serve the workforce needs in the community, and the workforce training and education needed for the students.

VISIONARY MINDSET

"In the future successful managers will become futurists and visionaries by recognizing both the continuities and changes in the market [in this case disruptions created by the ten technologies] and by learning how to respond to them quickly and effectively" (Millett, 2011, p. 234). Although Stephen Millett was writing for business leaders, his insight is just as true for those leading community colleges in the twenty-first century. Presidents will need to have a future-focused, visionary mindset in order to successfully lead the institution.

DYNAMIC VISIONING

This visionary mindset is not a one-time thing; it must be a continuous, dynamic process over the tenure of the leader. Research into the impact of specific technologies that have the potential to disrupt the institution must be ongoing, in-depth, and accurate. Of course, making sure the community college is successfully operational in the present is important to current stakeholders, but accurately envisioning the future of the institution is just as critical for the success of all constituents.

GROWTH MINDSET

A complementary way of learning how to deal with the future is to use the insight of Dr. Carol Dweck, a Stanford University psychologist, described in her book, *Mindset: The New Psychology of Success; How We Can Learn to Fulfill Our Potential* (Dweck, 2006). Dweck's research supports her idea that having a growth mindset leads to success in life and careers:

> The growth mindset is based on the belief that your basic qualities are things you can cultivate through your own efforts. Although people may differ in every which way—in the initial talents and aptitudes, interests, or temperaments—everyone can change and grow through application and experience. (Dweck, 2006, p. 7)

Dweck's notions can be invaluable to the community college president, administration, faculty and staff as they lead the institution for benefit of all concerned, focusing on students, the business community, and local economic development. The concepts she espouses can encourage community college leaders to always be looking ahead to understand what is in the offing and making plans to deal with it before it encompasses their institution. Uber, Airbnb, and Amazon did not come out of nowhere. All were ideas that could have been just as well considered and developed by other American entrepreneurs. In fact, other organizations have later developed to share in the success of those three businesses. Some have succeeded, others have not.

CONCLUSION

The successful community college president will lead the institution directly toward the new technologies, and find ways to work with them for success of the students, faculty and staff, the business community, and the local economic development organizations. Being proactive, future-focused with a twenty-year vision, combined with a growth mindset, is a foundation that will support community college presidents to keep their institutions viable in a disruptive future.

It will take considerable effort supported by serious research to prepare everyone in the college and the external stakeholders to make certain that the community college remains a viable source of education and training for students, the business community, local economic development organizations, and the community at large. The twenty-first century, with its accelerating technology disruptions, will require creative thinking and considerable effort on the part of community college leadership.

CHAPTER 2 SUMMARY

- Looking forward into the next ten to twenty years, true leaders will be required to keep community colleges intact and viable in a period of accelerating change.
- In general, the issues facing the community college during the next two decades will stretch the current abilities of presidents, college administration, faculty, and staff tremendously.
- It will become obvious to all that the twenty-first century is developing very differently than the twentieth. Preparing for changes on all fronts will face community college leaders.
- Changes will be needed in terms of what is to be taught, how it should be learned, and how the instruction supports the rapidly changing business community.
- The presidents and other leaders in the community college must become future-focused.
- It will be very useful to lead in a different way, one described as back from the future.
- This vision must come from serious, continuous research into the development of each of the ten technologies.
- It is important to envision the college twenty years out, understand what the possibilities are, and then plan back to the present.
- When planning from the present to the future, the president and the college will be entangled in what is happening in the present.
- Rather, the president and those in leadership positions in the college must stretch their thinking supported with appropriate, in-depth research out to a point of twenty into the future.
- Using that vision, the school can then develop a dynamic planning process leading toward that vision.

- The planning may have to be modified as time goes by, but the leadership will have a foundation on which to work from in making sound decisions.
- Presidents will need to have a future-focused, visionary mindset in order to successfully lead the institution.
- This visionary mindset is not a one-time thing; it must be a continuous, dynamic process over the tenure of the leader.
- Dweck's notions can be invaluable to the community college president, administration, faculty and staff as they lead the institution for benefit of all concerned, focusing on students, the business community, and local economic development.
- Being proactive, and future-focused with a twenty-year vision, combined with a growth mindset, is a foundation that will support community college presidents to keep their institutions viable in a disruptive future.
- The twenty-first century, with its accelerating technology disruptions, will require creative thinking and considerable effort on the part of community college leadership.

Chapter 3

Business in an Exponential Age

As of this writing, some CEOs in the business community are continuing to operate with business as usual, which for all intents and purposes means they apparently are either unaware of the ten technologies facing them, or are ignoring them. Either of those reactions will lead to potential problems for the business and its stakeholders and customers. In *The Technology Fallacy: How People are the Real Key to Digital Transformation,* a possible reason that business leaders are either unaware or ignoring is described: "Executives may not understand enough about technology to make the changes or to understand the urgency necessary (Kane et al., 2019, p. 17).

BUSINESS LEADERS' REACTION TO THE TECHNOLOGIES

However, for the most part, business CEOs and their boards are paying close attention to how each technology that faces them is developing. They are researching where the technologies are in terms of approaching stage two, the exponential stage. They remember Uber and Airbnb, and do not want to be caught wondering from where an unusual competitor suddenly appeared. They not only want to see what technologies are coming, but they want to learn how they can use them for increased effectiveness and efficiency in their businesses. They know that even if they are not making plans for integrating the technologies into their business, their competition is busy doing so.

They do not want to be caught in the situation where the competition is using the technology to potentially push them to the side or, in worst case, into bankruptcy. Whether or not to utilize the appropriate twenty-first century technology is not the question. At stake is how rapidly and how efficiently the technology can become an integral part of the business. For the CEO who wants to learn more about which technologies will impact the business, researching the Internet is one place to begin. Another is using the algorithms at book sellers like Amazon or Barnes and Noble, which will provide access to many published books on the topics of what technologies exist and ideas about how a business could deal with them.

AUTONOMOUS CARS

Whatever the business involved, there is probably more than one of the ten technologies that will impact the business, which will need awareness, research, planning as to how to deal with it. Take the automotive industry, for example. As of this writing, almost all automotive manufacturers are looking forward to the time the autonomous car will become a practical reality. Today, totally self-driving cars are being developed and some are already in use in foreign countries as well as domestically. CEOs in the automobile industry cannot ignore or be unaware of this new type of vehicle.

The big question is when will the autonomous car become a practical vehicle that is widely used throughout the country and the world? The answer to that issue has to do with when stage two, the exponential stage, will appear. It will take continual research and planning to determine when it will happen and be prepared to effectively use that shift in the car manufacturing world. No car manufacturer wants to be caught behind the eight ball in this situation. All want to be at the front edge of the development in order to benefit from the change.

Currently, as of the writing of this book, the federal government under President Biden is not only aware of the probabilities of electrically powered cars, but is making attempts through the media and actual legislation to promote funding for electric charging stations for electrically powered cars. That could be a first nationwide step to what will become the autonomous car in the next decade or sooner. Still in the making are safety regulations, insurance issues, and the question of how well the general population will be willing to accept autonomous cars. It did take a couple of decades for the gasoline powered car to fully replace horse-drawn vehicles.

THE INTERNET OF THINGS

The internet of things, using RFID sensors the size of a grain of rice inserted into or attached on all manufactured products, will send information from the product to the cloud by way of the internet. The sensors will provide bits of information about the mechanical, electric, and electronic segments of the product that can be accessed by the manufacturer, retailer, consumer, and others who are interested. That information will lead to improved products, increased sales, and clearer information for the consumer. The internet of things (IoT) holds tremendous potential for improvement and reliability of all products.

In addition, within a short period of time, the IoT will have sensors that not only send information to the cloud for access, but will also communicate with each other. For example, in the future, sensors within a refrigerator could keep track of all items, keep a list of what is running low, contact the super market, order replacements, pay for them, and arrange for transportation to the home involved. Information derived from sensors will also be used by entrepreneurs to create new businesses that analyze the information and communicate it to interested parties. The IoT is developing currently and soon will become a new normal in twenty-first century life and work.

IOT AND THE TESLA CAR

The Tesla car is a good example of how IoT can work in an automobile. Sensors are inserted and/or attached to many of the operating functions of the car. The sensors send bits of information to the cloud from many different parts of the car, which can be accessed by the manufacturer to discover how well the design and engineering of the parts perform. This is of obvious help to the manufacturer who can foresee issues that will arise and can be replaced and upgraded depending on the situation. Further, at times Tesla can actually repair a design issue virtually using the internet to make a repair without the owner having to do anything.

As the IoT grows in the cloud, entrepreneurs will see business possibilities in analyzing data and selling the findings to manufacturers, retailers, and consumers who may be interested. The potential business opportunities are considerable and will develop as the possibilities become understood. Undoubtedly, new businesses will spring up that are not even imagined at present. All it will take is some inventive thinking that will bring new ways to do things that are not currently considered. Remember Uber, Airbnb, and Amazon. The possibility was there for some time before some inventive thinking brought them into reality.

3D PRINTING (ADDITIVE MANUFACTURING)

3D printing, also known as additive manufacturing, is a process that could impact housing construction in a big way when it hits stage two. With additive manufacturing, the exterior walls, interior walls, and roofs can be printed with special kinds of concrete. An entire house can be constructed in less than a week, at much lower costs than current construction practices, and with exterior walls and roofs strong enough to withstand low category hurricanes.

This type of home construction, already used to some degree in Mexico and China, could provide tremendous assistance to subdivisions of homes that are annually ravaged by tornadoes, blown away with hurricanes, incinerated by forest fires, and swept away with floods. With current construction methods, it takes months to years to rebuild the homes that were destroyed. Additive manufacturing could rebuild the homes in weeks to months with construction that can better withstand the powerful forces of tornadoes, hurricanes, and fires. Furthermore, the construction process is considerably less expensive to rebuild.

ADDITIVE MANUFACTURING HOUSING

China has been developing additive manufactured prototypes from single family homes to multistory office complexes. It has found that entire houses can be constructed in a matter of a week. Further, multistory buildings can also be constructed in less than half the time of normal construction. Mexico is developing additive manufactured homes in subdivisions for low-income families. In the United States, a number of construction companies are beginning to develop prototypes that could be built in the very near future. When stage two is reached, additive manufactured housing will be implemented with exponential speed.

The potential for additive manufacturing to move into home construction is tremendous. It will take a mindset change as to how a house is usually constructed, but the decreased costs, stronger construction, and the increased speed of rebuilding could impact the housing industry significantly. The pre-cut lumber homes developed by Sears and Roebuck in the early twentieth century, which arrived almost anywhere in the United States by rail, created the construction of less expensive homes in rural and urban areas. Many those homes are still standing today.

CRISPR-CAS9

In healthcare, genome development with CRISPR-Cas9 provides the medical world with the potential of methods to cure of diseases that have plagued the world for decades. CRISPR-Cas9 provides the medical practitioner with the ability to move genes, delete genes, and insert genes into the human being. Compared to anything useable historically, this process is a potential game-changer. The possibilities are seemingly endless. Sickle cell anemia, cancer, heart disease, and a host of other medical ailments are already being researched to see how working with the genome can help to cure what today seem to be incurable medical problems.

DESIGNER BABIES

On top of cures for current ailments, the possibility will exist to create designer babies with none of the negative issues of their ancestors. It could allow for new physical strengths, attractive facial features, increased mental acuity, and much more. With further research, the cure for aging may be found and implemented. The possibilities are enormous in scope and only time stands between what is normal now and what will be the new normal in the future. "When it comes to CRISPR, the possibilities of this new technology—good and bad—are limited only by our imaginations" (Doudna, 2016, p. 240).

CRISPR AND AGRICULTURE

In the world of agricultural genome development, fruits and vegetables will attain increased vitality and length of time before spoiling. Animals will contain more meat and less fat. Growth rates of plants and animals will increase significantly. Disease in plants and animals will be reduced and, in many cases, eradicated. Food will become more tasteful and hold more nutrients. Again, the possibilities for improvement are significant. Further, the speed at which gene changes can be made is increased significantly, and the results can be observed in a fraction of the time needed previously.

Even if the population of the earth increases significantly, the food supply will be able to grow with it and beyond. The ability to modify agricultural products in terms of plants and animals will provide the path to keeping the food supply for human beings adequate and, most likely, ahead of the increasing needs. The beginnings of the research to improve the food supply for all those on the earth are already under way. In agriculture, the ability to use genes to create the improvements will be able to happen much more rapidly than modifying genes in human beings to fight off disease.

VERTICAL FARMING

As a side note, some countries are already experimenting with vertical farming. A vertical farm is a completely enclosed facility with multiple floors that grow plants in water under ideal conditions. The heat, light, fertilization, and other conditions are controlled using computer algorithms that make sure proper conditions are provided as the plants grow to maturity. This method of growing agricultural grains, vegetables, and other foodstuffs will also use genomic improvements in growing conditions that are not affected by the weather.

This method of farming could bring foodstuffs close to urban areas where farmland is being reduced annually as metropolitan areas expand.

In some states where large manufacturing plants stand idle because of competition from foreign countries, vertical farming could make use of those facilities at lower costs than constructing a new facility. This method of raising crops may become the new norm in the future. Again, computer and algorithms will control the environment of the facility. Stage two may raise its head in this area as well as so many others.

BITCOIN/BLOCKCHAIN

Bitcoin/Blockchain, an alternative to the current banking processes, continues with up and down levels of acceptance. It still is not completely accepted in the financial world, let alone by consumers. However, some changes may be seen in the near future such as the breakup of bitcoin and blockchain. The reason for that is bitcoin works with a finite worth of money. Although that amount used may sound like a great deal of money, in the world of finance, it is a limiting factor.

Blockchain, on the other hand, is a contract process that could work with bitcoin and other cyber-monetary types as well. It could be used with or without a cyber monetary format. The concerns about Bitcoin/Blockchain may forestall the monetary system from ever becoming useful; however, if the problems it faces can be solved, it has great potential in the United States and internationally. It could completely revise the current financial and contract system currently in existence.

ARTIFICIAL INTELLIGENCE

Artificial intelligence (AI) currently exists as what is called narrow AI. Its operation can be observed in Amazon, which uses algorithms to recommend books and/or products it determines will be of interest to the specific customer based on previous purchases. Narrow AI won chess matches with Gary Kasparov, one of the premier chess players in the world. It also has been used in the medical world to assist physicians to diagnose and provide prognoses for patients with serious diseases. The business world has found use of narrow AI as well in many applications such as automobile selection and purchase. The potential for AI in the business world is phenomenal.

AI FROM NARROW TO ARTIFICIAL GENERAL INTELLIGENCE

However, there is a caution in that AI can also be used to create the equivalent of a human mind, supposedly in all ways from decision making to emotional responses. Moore's law, in which the numbers of transistors on a chip doubles every eighteen months, if continued for about two more decades, would allow for an artificial general intelligence (AGI) mind to be created by 2045 (Kurzweil, 2005). Quantum computing, with an operational model announced by Google in September 2019, would increase the computing speed beyond anything currently described by the term exponential. Futurists predict that it could make the AGI mind possible by 2030. How the AGI will be used by countries or businesses is yet to be determined.

NANOTECHNOLOGY

Nanotechnology allows products to be manufactured using atoms. It is a difficult and somewhat dangerous process that demands an almost absolute zero temperature environment within which to operate. On the other hand, its potential is truly game-changing for the manufacturing world. In fact, when the process is fully implemented, every country in the world, with the proper environment and trained technicians, could make any product it would choose, and sell it on the open market. The country would need no natural resources, only atoms. There are already businesses working to develop this technology, but best estimates are that it will take until the mid-2040s for this technology to reach stage two and be fully implemented.

QUANTUM COMPUTING

The tenth technology for consideration is quantum computing. This type of computing uses atoms rather than transistors to operate. It literally miniaturizes everything in the digital world. For example, if all the data ever produced on today's classical computers were stored in one place, it is estimated that it would take a multistoried facility some six blocks long to contain it all. That same amount of data in a quantum computer would take up the space of one half of a period at the end of the sentence. The speed of the quantum computer is so fast that it makes the speed of Moore's law look like it is going in reverse.

MERGERS

Combinations of AI and nanotechnology, AI and quantum computing, nanotechnology and quantum computing, and a merger of the three, all of which are possible, go beyond game changers for life as it is known today. There would appear to be no limits with the exception of the universe itself. Everything *Star Trek*, *Star Wars*, and such like science fiction have designed would have the potential of becoming science fact. When these three technologies reach stage two, the exponential stage, all predictions and forecasts are pretty much off the table. A new world may exist. Maybe a new universe.

A question might be, how does the business community keep up with and use all these developing technologies for the good of mankind. What will the impact be? When will the impacts arrive? Most likely in the lifetime of anyone born in the year 2000 or after will learn the answers to those questions. From an optimistic perspective, the twenty-first century has the potential to be vastly different from anything mankind has experienced in the past. Problems and issues facing the human race have the potential to be solved. From a pessimistic perspective, things could get really serious. Those living through the twenty-first century will have unprecedented situations to live with and work through.

CONCLUSION

Looking back through history, humans have often faced seemingly impossible situations including food shortages, ice ages, the black plague, world wars, and today, climate change for some obvious examples. In all cases, the human race has worked through the situations, journeyed on, and did not disappear from our planet. Looking forward, recall that issues in the past were often much less dangerous than they first appeared. "Technology has always created more jobs even as it destroys them, and in the past, it has tended to create more jobs than it eliminates" (Merisotis, 2020, p. 5). Those living through the twenty-first century must remain optimistic, no matter what, and help to create a successful future for all concerned.

CHAPTER 3 SUMMARY

- For the most part, business CEOs and their boards are paying very close attention to how each technology that faces them is developing.
- They know that even if they are not making plans for integrating the technology into their business, their competition is.
- For the CEO who may want to learn more about which technologies will impact the business, researching the internet is one place to begin.
- Whatever the business involved, there is probably one or more of the ten technologies that will impact the business, which will need research, awareness, and planning as to how to deal with it.
- The big question is when will the autonomous car become a practical vehicle that is widely used throughout the country and the world?
- IoT holds tremendous potential for improvement and reliability of all products.
- In addition, within a short period of time, the IOT will have sensors that not only send information to the cloud for access, but will also communicate with each other.
- The Tesla car is a good example of how IoT can work in an automobile.
- As the IoT grows in the cloud, most likely entrepreneurs will see business possibilities in analyzing data and selling the findings to manufacturers, retailers, and consumers who may be interested.
- 3D printing, also known as additive manufacturing, is a process that will impact housing construction in a big way when it hits stage two.
- China has been developing prototypes from single family homes to multistory office complexes.

- Mexico is developing additive manufactured homes in subdivisions for low-income families.
- Currently, when a hurricane hits an off-shore island or comes on land and destroys homes, business facilities, schools, and other constructed buildings, it often takes years to rebuild what was destroyed.
- Rather than waiting for years to rebuild communities, new homes and business structures can be completed in a matter of weeks at considerably lower costs than those being replaced.
- In healthcare, genome development with CRISPR-Cas9 provides the medical world with the potential for cures of diseases that have plagued the world for decades. Compared to anything useable historically, this process is a potential game-changer.
- The possibilities are enormous in scope and only time stands between what is normal now and what will be the new normal in the future.
- In the world of agricultural genome development, fruits and vegetables will attain increased vitality and length of time before spoiling.
- Further, the speed at which gene changes can be made is increased significantly and the results can be observed in a fraction of the time that was needed previously.
- Even if the population of the earth increases significantly, the food supply will grow with it and possibly beyond.
- The beginnings of the research to improve the food supply for all those on the earth are already under way.
- As a side note, some countries are already experimenting with vertical farming.
- This method of growing agricultural grains, vegetables, and other foodstuffs will also use genomic improvements in growing conditions that are not affected by the weather.
- Bitcoin/Blockchain continues up and down levels of acceptance. It still is not completely accepted in the financial world, let alone by consumers.
- Artificial intelligence (AI) currently exists in what is called Narrow AI.
- The potential for AI in the business world is phenomenal.

- However, there is a danger in that AI can also be used to create the equivalent of a human mind, supposedly in all ways from decision making to emotional responses.
- How artificial general intelligence (AGI) will be used by business is yet to be determined.
- Nanotechnology allows products to be manufactured using atoms.
- In fact, when the process is fully implemented, every country in the world, with the proper environment and trained operators, could make any product it would choose, and sell it on the open market.
- The tenth technology for consideration is quantum computing. This type of computing uses atoms rather than transistors to operate.
- The speed of the quantum computer is so fast that it makes the speed of Moore's law look like it is going in reverse.
- When these the technologies (artificial intelligence, nanotechnology, and quantum computing) reach stage two, the exponential stage, all predictions and forecasts are pretty much off the table.
- The twenty-first century has the potential to be vastly different from anything mankind has experienced in the past.
- Looking back through history, humans have often faced seemingly impossible situations including food shortages, ice ages, the black plague, world wars, and climate change for some obvious examples.
- In all cases, the human race has journeyed on and did not disappear.
- Remain optimistic, no matter what, and help to create the successful future for all concerned.

Chapter 4

Seven Technologies

Historically, community colleges have been in a fast-follow mode with the business community. Well-trained work forces, developed at reasonable costs from the 1920s on to the present, have worked well using that mode. As most community college presidents understand things at present, what worked well in the past century should continue on in the twenty-first. But, is that true? Back in the mid-twentieth century, University of Michigan anthropologist, Marshall Sahlins (1960) made the following observation, "Ideological systems, too, are inherently conservative and backward looking, deriving their authority and sanction from the conditions of the past" (Sahlins and Service, 1960, p. 54). His observation may remain true for community college leadership today.

PAST VS. FUTURE

It is easy for today's community college president to continue to use what worked well and made sense in the past. However, the foundation for today's community college, designed by William Rainey Harper with the Junior College, was often modified in the twentieth century to meet the needs of American society during the Great Depression, World War II, the Cold War, and baby boomers. Now in the twenty-first century, community colleges are approaching the need for more very serious changes. The community college today will need to morph into something more than it ever was previously. Presidents of the successful community college movement to serve the higher educational needs of recent high school graduates and adults will soon feel the impact of ten twenty-first century technologies.

STAGE TWO

These ten technologies will need to be understood, planned for, and appropriate action must be taken to deal with what is coming with effectiveness for all concerned in the community college movement including faculty, staff, board members, the business community, elected officials, community leaders, and most of all, the students. The work-world of the next thirty years will not be a reflection of the previous decades. The ten technologies of the twenty-first century, most of which, if not all, will reach stage two, the exponential stage, between 2025 and 2050. If stage two of any of these technologies is similar to the experience of Uber or Airbnb, they will seem to appear out of nowhere to those who are not aware.

SEVEN TECHNOLOGIES

This chapter will discuss seven of the ten technologies: autonomous vehicles, the internet of things, 3D printing, medical genome development, agricultural genome development, personal robots, and Bitcoin/Blockchain. The other three, the big elephants in the room, artificial intelligence, nanotechnology, and quantum computing, will be discussed in chapter 5. Each technology will be discussed in terms of what disruptions it will bring and how it can be dealt with in the community college. "The robots might or might not be coming to take our jobs, but it's clear that society is being thrust into a new era of human work: the work only humans can do in an age of smart machines" (Merisotis, 2020, p. viii).

AUTONOMOUS AUTOMOBILES

"In April 2015, the first driverless car to cross the United States arrived at its destination in Manhattan after nine days" (Willyerd et al., 2016,

p. 12). Autonomous cars are on the horizon, most likely to hit stage two in the late 2020s or early 2030s. All major car companies are currently in the design stages of development. Many have already built prototype self-driving cars, others are not far behind, and all of them understand the interest in this type of automobile. In addition, companies like Apple and Google are also in the mix, designing or constructing actual self-driving cars. All are leading toward what will be a significant disruption in the automobile world.

Most likely the autonomous car will develop simultaneously with the electrically powered car, which could disrupt things even more. A segment of the oil industry would be phased out over a period of years, which would create issues in dealerships, gas stations, car repair and the like. However, even if the autonomous automobiles were designed with gasoline engines, they will significantly disrupt the maintenance and repair processes.

Since many community colleges offer automotive programs, they will have to adapt to the needs of this new type of vehicle. Administrators, automotive department heads, and faculty will need to become aware of what is coming, when it is most likely will arrive, and what will need to be changed in the automotive curriculum, equipment, and facilities.

Impact on Faculty

The autonomous automobile will require upgrading and retraining of the faculty on how to repair and maintain this type of vehicle. Constant research into the development of this type of vehicle will be required, followed by planning as to what will be needed in terms of equipment, faculty training, and facilities. The disruption will most likely require additional funding and resources. The college will need to be prepared for the disruption, if the institution desires to remain viable for the training that will be needed.

It is true that the automotive programs have in the past gone through significant changes brought on by the functions that were computerized during the 1980s. Almost overnight the carburetor was replaced, the electrical components became computerized, and many mechanical connections were replaced by electronic ones. As a result, those teaching in the automotive programs needed additional training and upgrading. Experience with that change process may make it more reasonable to understand what will need to be done to train faculty to be able to successfully handle the maintenance and repair of the autonomous car.

THE INTERNET OF THINGS

Expectations for the internet of things (IoT) to hit stage two is sometime in the mid-2020s. IoT has been in existence for a number of years. RFID sensors, placed on or in manufactured products, send information to the cloud, and have been doing so for some time. It is expected that there will soon be trillions of bits of information in storage, waiting to be accessed, analyzed, and used.

Some manufacturers are already making use of the information that pertains to their products determining the lifespan, its strengths and weaknesses, and acceptance by the consumer. "[It's] easy to see how IoT will impact every major industry: healthcare; financial systems; transportation; energy production; transmission and distribution; agriculture; smart city services; the list is endless (Schwab, 2018, p. 103).

Impact on the Community College

The community college will soon be developing courses and maybe entire programs to train those already in existing businesses using the IoT and preparing those about to enter the workforce of the businesses. But that is just the tip of the iceberg. Entrepreneurs will be investigating how to get involved with the analysis of the information collected and how to determine the market for information that would be beneficial to existing manufacturers, retailers and consumers. In the near future, the IoT could make transparency a byword for any product or service from development to implementation.

The potential of the IoT for courses and programs at the community college is significant. It needs to be continually researched to understand when the IoT will reach stage two and explode onto the scene. Existing businesses will need their employees upgraded and new employees will need to be taught skills to deal with the IoT brought into the businesses. The potential is developing behind the scenes and must be researched before it spills onto the scene with the velocity of Uber, Airbnb, or Amazon.

3D PRINTING (ADDITIVE MANUFACTURING)

3D printing (3DP), or additive manufacturing (AM), is beginning to generate businesses in many diverse areas both in the United States and abroad. This can be observed on the internet where many businesses are already advertising their various products. Although the technology has not yet gone exponential, it is developing in a number of countries. This development will only increase because the 3DP and AM are useful in so many areas of business. Further, both are considerably less expensive than current methods and they produce products much more rapidly.

Those businesses not paying attention will find themselves wondering how so many successful 3D and AM businesses suddenly appeared. When 3D and AM hit the exponential stage, the businesses involved will rapidly move ahead of those manufacturing businesses which attempt to hold onto the status quo. Uber, Airbnb, and Amazon demonstrate what happens when existing, even thriving businesses, are not paying attention to what their competitors are doing. It is best not be caught unaware. Again, be sure local research is being conducted to inform the community college leaders when 3D printing and additive manufacturing reach stage two.

Foreign Implementation

The additive manufacturing process of home construction must be carefully and consistently followed. China has jumped ahead with the process and already developed prototypes of single-family homes and multistory buildings that be constructed in a matter of days at cost far below standard stick-built homes and facilities. Further, the outside walls and roof of the house or facility are able to withstand hurricane winds of the lower categories. When stage two is reached, countries which have regions devastated by hurricanes, floods, tornadoes, or forest fires can much more rapidly rebuild the homes and commercial facilities that were severely damaged.

Home Use

In addition, current estimates indicate that 3D printing within the home will become as universal as the personal computer. Basically, homeowners will be able to create products that wear out or for some reason need replacement or upgrade. Just as the personal computer began as a business device, which received great skepticism when introduced in the 1980s, and developed into a product used in both business and home use; so, the 3D printer is expected to become as widespread in the next few years.

House Construction

The impact on manufacturing could be significant by the early 2030s, when 3D printing reaches stage two. Additive manufactured houses and multistory facilities could disrupt the construction business. Stronger, longer lasting, less expensive homes could take over the market. As of this writing, in Mexico entire subdivisions are being developed using additive manufacturing for families of lower income. In the United States, there are some companies looking seriously at beginning AM housing in subdivisions. By the early 2030s additive-manufactured houses could become the new standard for home construction.

Impact on the Community College

It is expected that a 3D printer as a household item will become as widespread as the personal computer. The ability to repair items, rebuild items and creatively develop new items will be at the fingertips of most everyone. When 3D printing becomes a household item, there will be plenty of opportunities for continuing education courses to teach community members how to use them most effectively. 3D printing will bring new opportunities to the community college in terms of new courses and programs.

Additive manufacturing will present another opportunity, that of a program to teach house construction. Since additive manufacturing allows house construction to be considerably faster than convention methods, greatly reduces in cost to build, and provides a house that is much stronger to the point where it can sustain high winds, it has the potential to become a revolutionary method to provide housing. The community college can be at the forefront for training in this new method. Further, additive manufacturing may open doors to innovative ways of construction of other things that will require training at the community college level.

MEDICAL GENOME DEVELOPMENT

Dr. Jennifer Doudna, with the support and help of French scientist Dr. Emmanuelle Charpentier, was able to bring into existence a biological process now known as CRISPR-Cas9. Their understanding of this powerful method allowed them to open a door in the medical genome world to do three things with genes: to move them, to insert them, and to delete them in the genome. The door they opened, which Doudna describes in considerable detail in her book, *A Crack in Creation: Gene Editing and the Unthinkable Power to Control Evolution*, allowed for making changes in the genome directly (Doudna and Sternberg, 2017).

CRISPR-Cas9 and the Medical World

As a result, any disease that is created or affected by the genome could be modified by making changes in the genome itself. Suddenly, there are a number of diseases troubling mankind that have the potential to be literally done away with. Gene modification could be implemented individually with a person or be completed so that the change passed on from that person to his/her progeny, depending on how it is done.

In addition, CRISPR/Cas9 opened the real possibilities of creating designer children, who would not face the medical issues of their parents. It could change the normal gene process between mother and father to create a child with exceptional characteristics such as strength, beauty, increased intelligence, and more. The possibilities are extensive and most likely will be used by many parents in the coming decades.

Gene modification was a breakthrough so amazing and far-reaching that Dr. Doudna became fearful that the process might be used to create a superior race. As a result, she began speaking internationally to her colleagues and others about the fact that this process must be somehow controlled and used only for the good of mankind rather than the opposite (Doudna, 2017). How successful she will be in that attempt remains to be seen, as medically trained individuals world-wide could soon be able to use CRISPR-Cas9. This process has the potential to be a game-changer in the medical world.

Implications for Community Colleges

Medical personnel using the CRISPER/Cas9 method of genome capabilities will need staff to assist them with the patients and the procedures used. That need will bring the potential for courses and programs designed to train the assistants. As it is possible that the procedures for dealing with genome treatments will specialize, it will further provide community colleges with the development of courses and programs to meet the specialized medical community needs.

Agricultural Genome Development

Parallel to medical genome development, agricultural genome development will directly affect changes in plants, trees, vegetables, grains, livestock, and anything plant or animal related. Current concerns about a food shortage in the future could be totally taken care of by food plants that grow faster, contain more nutrients, spoil more slowly, and whatever else is needed to provide adequate food for the world population. Furthermore, it could be used with animals to produce meat with higher levels of protein, shorter growth spans, and increased shelf life. The potential is phenomenal.

Community colleges offering agriculture programs will be presented with the potential for revising current programs and developing new ones. Faculty will need upgraded training to meet the new program needs. Add in vertical farming, with plants being grown in a multistory facility with the interior environment completely controlled by computer algorithms, and the community college again will have a new program to train those involved with that method of agriculture. The possibilities are extensive.

PERSONAL ROBOTS

So far, personal robots are being developed in stage one, the linear fashion. Today there are robotic vacuum cleaners that can clean and wash floors. Alexa can control lighting, temperature, and security in the home as well as answer questions on the spot. Ring can show who is at the door and allow a conversation with that individual. It can show what is going on anywhere else in and around the home where a camera is placed, indoors or outside. These and other computer-controlled, robotic mechanisms are available on the market today. They are only the beginning.

Robots and Humans

Robots that look like human beings, walk and talk like them, are already being developed. The Japanese got into the personal robot industry in 2005 with ASIMO, a creation of Honda Motors. Japan is a set of mountainous islands with limited space for human living conditions. As a result, the government has very strict limits as to how many immigrants it will admit to the country. On the other hand, because of the healthy diet in the country, it tends to have a larger percentage of older citizens; so many in fact, that there are not nearly enough young persons to care for them in their later years.

Japanese Development

Consequently, the Japanese decided to develop personal robots to serve the needs of the aging population. As a result, they are far ahead in the design, production, and testing of robots to meet that need. They have gone so far as to develop robots that have human characteristics including physical looks, human-like movement, ability to assist others, talk, and so on. For other reasons, China, South Korea, some European countries, and the United States have also gotten into the development of personal robots, so much so, that as of this writing, there are some very sophisticated personal robots already in existence.

Robots Everywhere

Where is this technology going? Stage two is expected in the mid-2030s. If that prediction is correct, personal robots to do housework, cooking, clothes-washing, lawn mowing, and most other in-home chores will be able to be purchased at retail stores, internet stores, and anywhere else products are bought and sold. This technology is growing at a rapid rate, again behind the scenes. When personal robots reach stage two, within a relatively short time they literally will be everywhere, and humans will have to adapt to them, which may be an easy task.

Impact on the Community College

As the number and type of personal robots increase in the home and business environments, there will be opportunities for training and education for the community college. Human beings will need to learn how to deal with robots in the home as they provide numerous repetitive tasks that will make like easier and more beneficial. In the business world, robots will provide repetitive tasks including receptionist, lawn mowing, housekeeping of the facilities, and security for the entire campus. The robots will need repair and maintenance to keep them operable and software development to assist them with their various tasks. The colleges will be soon be offering courses and programs to meet the needs of the homeowner and the business proprietor.

BITCOIN/BLOCKCHAIN

Cybercurrency such as Bitcoin is already on the scene and used on a daily basis in some international situations. However, Bitcoin/Blockchain continues to develop with up and down levels of acceptance. It has not disappeared, far from it, but it still is not completely accepted in the financial world. China has been more pro-Bitcoin/Blockchain than the United States, but even that is changing. However, China, the United States, or any other country may find ways to solve the issues that limit the current digital process and work out solutions. Whenever the issues facing Bitcoin/Blockchain are resolved, this cryptocurrency system of digital finances, could have international ramifications.

Changes in Banking and Community Colleges

If the Bitcoin/Blockchain technology reaches stage two, as is expected in the early 2030s, it has the potential to seriously disrupt the banking world to the point where banks might go out of business, or become institutions very different from what they are today. If Bitcoin/Blockchain becomes the standard monetary system, courses in current business curricula in the community college will need to make tremendous changes in their program offerings. The college itself will need to use the method for payment of tuition, fees, and other costs, which will modify the financial operation of the college.

CONCLUSION

As can be see thus far, these seven technologies stand to make some serious changes in the world in general and in community colleges as well. The community college president, administration, faculty, and staff will need to adapt to some disruptive changes that will call for action in terms of facilities, equipment, faculty, and programs. It appears that the disruptions could come one after the other, which makes it so critically important that college leadership, faculty, staff, board members, business leaders, and, most of all students, are kept up to date on what is going on behind the scenes, be able to accurately predict when the disruptions are most likely to happen, and how the college is planning to deal with them.

The internet of things may move to stage two by the mid-2020s. Autonomous vehicles and quantum computing may move to stage two by the late 2020s. Artificial intelligence, 3D printing/additive manufacturing, Bitcoin/Blockchain, and medical and agricultural genome development may move to stage two by the early 2030s. Personal robots may move to stage two by the mid-2030s, and nanotechnology by the mid-2040s.

CHAPTER 4 SUMMARY

- Historically, community colleges have been in a fast-follow mode with the business community.
- As near as most community college presidents understand things at present, what worked well in the past century should continue on in the twenty-first.

- The community college today will need to morph into something more than it ever was previously.
- The work-world of the next thirty years will not be a reflection of the previous three decades.
- If stage two of any of these technologies is similar to the experience of Uber or Airbnb, they will seem to appear out of nowhere to those not aware and prepared.
- To begin with, autonomous cars are on the horizon, most likely to hit stage two in the late 2020s or early 2030s.
- Since many community colleges offer automotive programs, they will have to adapt to the needs of the new type of vehicle.
- It will require faculty being upgraded and retrained on how to repair and maintain these types of vehicles.
- IoT has been in existence for a number of years. Sensors placed on or in manufactured products, which can by RFID send information to the cloud, have been doing so for some time.
- The community college will soon be developing courses and maybe entire programs to train those already in existing businesses using the IoT and preparing those about to enter the workforce of the businesses.
- In the near future, the IoT could make transparency a byword for any product from development to implementation.
- The potential of the IoT for courses and programs at the community college is significant.
- 3D printing (3DP) or additive manufacturing (AM) is beginning to generate businesses in many diverse areas both in the United States and abroad.
- Those businesses not paying attention will find themselves wondering how so many successful 3D and AM businesses suddenly appeared.
- The additive manufacturing process of home construction must be carefully and consistently followed.
- Additive manufacturing will present another opportunity, that of a program to teach house construction.
- It is expected that a 3D printer as a household item will become as widespread as the personal computer.

- Dr. Jennifer Doudna, with the support and help of French scientist Dr. Emmanuelle Charpentier, was able to bring into existence a biological process now known as CRISPR-Cas9.
- As a result, any disease affected by the genome could be modified by making changes in the genome itself.
- This process has the potential to be a game-changer in the medical world.
- Parallel to medical genome development, agricultural genome development will directly affect changes in plants, trees, vegetables, grains, and anything plant related.
- Medical personnel using the CRISPER/Cas9 method of genome capabilities will need staff to assist them with the patients and the procedures used.
- So far, personal robots have arrived only in a stage one, linear fashion.
- Robots that look like human beings, walk like them, and talk like them are already being developed.
- China, South Korea, some European countries, and the United States have also gotten into the act, so much so that as of this writing, there are some pretty sophisticated personal robots that already exist.
- When personal robots reach stage two, within a relatively short time, they literally will be everywhere and humans will have to adapt to them.
- The robots will need repair and maintenance to keep them operable and software development to assist them with their various tasks.
- The colleges will be soon offering courses and programs to meet the needs of the homeowner and the business proprietor.
- Cybercurrency such as Bitcoin is already on the scene and used on a daily basis in some situations internationally.
- If Bitcoin/Blockchain becomes the standard monetary system, courses in current business curricula in the community college will need to make tremendous changes in their program offerings.
- The community college president, administration, faculty, and staff will need to adapt to disruptive changes that will call for action in terms of facilities, equipment, faculty, and programs.

Chapter 5

The Big Three Technologies

There are three big elephants in the room: nanotechnology, artificial intelligence and quantum computing. Any one of the three has the potential to be extremely disruptive to business, education, health fields, and life in general; while on the other hand, they create new possibilities that are extremely supportive and useful. Taken together, the three provide potential for both extremely powerful disruptions and/ or phenomenally beneficial changes. It will be the college leadership, starting with the president along with administrators, faculty, staff and board, who will decide which directions the institution will travel.

THE ROAD AHEAD

It will not be an easy journey. It will be filled with a variety of possibilities that lead to success or failure. By the second half the twentieth century, community college presidents found the highways that led to success for the college. Obviously, those in leadership will be interested in finding ways to integrate these three technologies into the operation of the college to remain viable and useful to students, faculty, staff, administrators, the business community, and local economic development. In simplest terms, community college presidents will need to learn to how to deal with these technologies or the technologies will deal with them.

The previous seven technologies discussed in chapter 4, may provide sharp curves in the road; however, they can be driven through with careful, well-prepared, deliberate effort. They will impact the institution, some more, some less, but they are reasonable to understand and adapt to. While keeping the college in the middle of the lane with the first seven technologies is possible with some hard work, the three technologies discussed in this chapter, will take time and effort beyond what is reasonable. It will take more than any successful community college president has experienced before and more than he or she ever thought they would have to deal with.

THE BIG THREE AND THE BUSINESS COMMUNITY

It is clear that CEOs in the business world will have to deal with these three big elephants as well. They will have to learn how to work with them, how to integrate them, and how to use them in order to remain competitive in the global business world. As they make their way through the potential morass of disruptions heading their way, successful business leaders may be able to provide considerable encouragement and support to community college presidents. Since community colleges provide training for the workforce required in the business community, it will be wise to keep an eye out for how local businesses are making their way.

THE BIG THREE AND THE COMMUNITY COLLEGE

On the other hand, the community college may at times move ahead more rapidly than business leaders in learning how to integrate the technologies and will be of assistance and support to the business community. The big three elephants put business leaders and community college leaders in the same technology boat. It would behoove both types of leaders to work together as much as possible. The ride may be rough at times, but with creative and innovative thinking, both the college and the business community, can assist each other in getting successfully through the dangerous pathways.

NANOTECHNOLOGY

Of the three big elephants, nanotechnology most likely will not reach stage two before 2040–2045. In the meantime, there will be a great deal of developmental work behind the scenes that may not receive much wide-spread attention. That is good from the perspective of the community college president, since it gives the leader time to get prepared. Nanotechnology falls under the category of manufacturing, and it brings to the table a construction method of almost anything that is totally different from any being currently used. Nanotechnology is a method of constructing things, not using plastic, steel, wood, concrete, fiberglass, or any combination of them. Rather, it uses atoms to construct products.

The Past of Nanotechnology

Nanotechnology has actually been around awhile, dating back to the early 1980s, with ideas about it going back to the 1950s. There have been some start-up businesses that have tried to get into nanotechnology; some have failed, and others continue. The development of this technology is not one that will soon jump into the collective consciousness. It will continue to develop mostly behind the scenes with little fanfare for some time.

Working with atoms, nanotechnology operates where the laws developed by Isaac Newton do not exist. Instead, it develops in the quantum world where nothing works as it does in the observable world. Not even close. Quantum physics has discovered that atoms exist in two places at the same time. They can be close to each other or extremely far apart. No matter the distance, they stay connected to each other. That may sound ridiculous because things do not work that way in the observable world in which Newton's laws work quite well.

Issues in the Nanotechnology World

The quantum world of atoms and molecules is not an easy or safe place to work. First, extreme cold is needed, almost absolute zero. Second, working with atoms can be dangerous as they can move into and out of a human body with no problem. On the other hand, there is the potential for transforming our world, and maybe parts of the universe itself.

Nanotechnology is in stage one developing at a fairly slow pace. When it might reach stage two has been estimated to be about 2040–2045. When it does move to stage two, the effects on the community college would be tremendous and difficult to envision.

New Possibilities

In the quantum world, since operational nanotechnology would be able to create anything out of atoms, there would be no shortage of natural resources. Products could be constructed, and the poorest nations, with the proper equipment and trained personnel could find themselves able to compete globally on whatever profit-making products they would like to pursue. Wealth could be completely redefined as every country would be on an even playing field in terms of construction. Nanotechnology could be a world-changer.

Impact for Community Colleges

How nanotechnology will affect community colleges is truly hard to determine. If training facilities can be constructed on campuses, there will certainly be a grand variety of courses and most likely a series of programs to train students to work in the various segments this unusual environment. Just because it is difficult to envision, does not mean that community colleges will not be involved in training and education of employees working in the nanotechnology arena. Undoubtedly methods and procedures will be developed that will require highly trained individuals. Community colleges will no doubt meet the needs.

ARTIFICIAL TECHNOLOGY

Artificial technology (AI) is already prominent in the world today. Some obvious examples are Siri and Alexa, which are known as narrow AI. They can provide certain processes such as answering a wide spectrum of questions, turning on the lights, playing particular types of music, and/or changing the temperature in a room. Amazon uses algorithms to search out products a consumer might want by analyzing past purchases. In addition, AI allows Tesla cars to ride on the open road with ease with little attention from the driver. There are multiple uses of narrow artificial technology in the early twenty-first century world, and the number is increasing every day.

Narrow AI Benefits

As long as artificial technology remains narrow and specific, it will do much to enhance the lives of human beings. Adaptations of the Watson computer in the medical world assist the physician in diagnosing disease and recommending best practices and procedures. In the agricultural arena it will help the farmer to decide on what to plant, when to irrigate the crop, how to go about fertilizing the crops, and where to successfully sell the harvest for the best price point. There is no end to the way narrow AI can assist and support life on the planet. It will depend on the creative and innovative thinking of human beings.

AI Issues

However, there is another side to AI development. In the mid-1960s, Gordon Moore, one of Intel's leaders, began to understand that the number of transistors on a chip was increasing significantly each year. He surmised that the development seemed to be doubling every year; a few years later he changed that cycle to every two years, and a bit later, he decided that the more accurate number was that it doubled every eighteen months. That eighteen-month increase has remained fairly consistent over the years and decades. So much so, that by 2021, the equivalence of 2.6 trillion transistors were placed on a chip.

That kind of increase got futurist Ray Kurzweil figuring out that if the doubling continued, it would be possible to create a computer mind equal in all areas, from IQ to emotions, in the mind of a human being (Kurzweil, 2005). He and other futurists envisioned a computer they called artificial general intelligence (AGI), which it was decided could become a reality in 2045. Further, it was predicted that the computer-based AGI would have an IQ of approximately 600. That computer, if small enough, could be inserted into the head of a robot, or, if that was not possible, it could be connected to a robot wirelessly. Either way would create a robot which would have a mind equivalent to a human being.

A computer and/or robot with a mind like a human with an IQ of 600 or so is a bit frightening to say the least. But the computer power and appropriate algorithms could make it possible. An artificial general intelligent robot provided nightmare visions for scientists, military leaders, computer geeks, and others who became knowledgeable about it. For the sake of argument, if the number of transistors on a chip continued to double for the three to five years after the initial artificial general intelligence was created, another type of computer mind would develop, that of an artificial super computer (ASI) with a mental IQ in the millions. That computer mind, if small enough, could be placed in a robot, or if too large, it too could be connected wirelessly to the robot.

Moore's Law and AGI and ASI

According to Moore's Law, all that could happen by 2045–2050. To nudge the scenario further, if one ASI could be developed, how about two, or ten or a thousand? The nightmare situation grows, exponentially. Questions could arise as to the need for human beings in a robot-run world, or perhaps, robot governed galaxy, or beyond. The computer mind of AGI or ASI is called a singularity. How close is that kind of being? Today, ever closer that one might think. Quantum computing, first completed in 2019, throws Moore's Law out the window. The speed and storage capability of quantum computing, which uses atoms instead of transistors on a silicon chip, leaves Moore's Law in the far behind in the dust.

Quantum Computing and AGI/ASI

Narrow artificial technology, which exists today in many forms, could with quantum computing power morph into artificial general intelligence by 2030 using the power of quantum computing. And artificial super intelligence would follow rapidly behind. Would the leaders in the United States stop the development of AGI and ASI from happening? Would that move be wise? Probably not, as other countries on the planet could make it happen. The best route would most likely be to support the development to keep the country from falling far behind and finding itself in a dangerous position as the AGI and ASI intellect would undoubtedly be used by the military.

It is quite obvious that artificial intelligence will soon contain computer power that could be used for the great benefit of mankind or the possible demise of the human race. If those two routes were a millennium away, sitting back and resting easy today would be a reasonable thing to do. However, if those two paths, benefit or demise, are coming within ten years or so. Ignoring the possibility is nonsensical and extremely dangerous. The leaders in community colleges will need to know what is coming, when it is coming, how to plan for it, and what actions to take.

Implication for Community Colleges

It will all depend on whether AGI/ASI are able to be controlled by humankind. If the AGI/ASI mind placed into the head of a robot operates using man-made algorithms with limits placed on their abilities to learn and develop, there will be possibilities for humankind and AGI/ASI robots to work together for the good of all concerned. Community colleges will be a part of that world. If the AGI/ASI mentality is developed in an uncontrolled manner, with no limits on the mental abilities to learn and develop, community colleges could find themselves in a world where it is of little or no use, a terrible consequence of allowing AGI/ASI to rule the planet.

QUANTUM COMPUTING

If two elephants in the room are not enough, there is the third, quantum computing. Working in the same quantum world in which nanotechnology operates, there are scientists who are developing computing, using atoms. Doing that puts those scientists into a totally different environment. At the quantum level, Newton's laws do not exist. However, scientists working in the quantum environment can take advantage of the fact that two atoms are connected no matter the distance. In the classical computer that is used daily, the processor works with bits. There are ones and zeros. Transistors handle that difference by turning off or on. In the quantum computer, the bits become quantum bits or qubits. A qubit is made up of a pair of atoms. Each atom has not one set of ones and zeros but a myriad of sets. That makes a phenomenal difference in how fast the computer can operate.

Quantum Computing is a Reality

Quantum computing is a game changer in the computer world. It opens up opportunities only imagined about in the past. Since computing has made its way into almost every academic discipline and all business environments, bringing an almost unbelievable increase in speed and data storage to the table, both academia and business will see phenomenal changes in the very near future. Following Google's announcement in September 2019 that it had successfully developed an operational quantum computer, IBM and other computer manufacturers were following close behind. Americans should be very pleased that the first one was created in the United States.

Foreign Countries and Quantum Computing

The Chinese are investing $10 billion in a four million square foot facility that will deal only with quantum metrology and quantum computing. The facility was originally planned to be completed in 2020. Most likely it exists today. And the Chinese are not the only ones interested in developing and using the benefits of quantum computing. European countries are close behind as well. Most likely Russia is in the game, although they are saying little to indicate their progress as of the writing of this book.

Implications for Community Colleges

As long as quantum computing only speeds up business, educational, health, government, and military processes, the community college will find many opportunities for training in the high velocity method of developing procedures, following up on them, and creating new ways to benefit mankind. However, if quantum computing is used in the development of AGI/ASI or nanotechnology with few or no algorithmic controls, the community college will find itself in a totally new world. Community college leaders must remain research oriented in order to be aware of what is facing education.

CONCLUSION

The three big elephants in the room as described in this chapter coexist with the seven twenty-first-century technologies discussed in chapter 4. These ten technologies should make it very clear that life in the twenty-first century will be filled with changes. All ten of technologies will reach stage two, exponential development, some within the current decade, and others to follow. Amazon, Uber, and Airbnb are harbingers of the speed, and wide spectrum of change can happen when that second stage is in effect.

CHAPTER 5 SUMMARY

- There are three big elephants in the room: nanotechnology, artificial intelligence, and quantum computing.
- Taken together, the three provide potential for both extremely powerful disruptions and/or phenomenal beneficial changes.
- In simplest terms, community college presidents will need to learn to how to deal with the technologies or the technologies will deal with them.
- The previous seven technologies discussed in chapter 4, may provide sharp curves in the road; however, they can be driven through with careful, well-prepared, deliberate effort.
- The three technologies discussed in this chapter, AI, nanotechnology, and quantum computing, will take time and effort beyond what is reasonable.
- As they make their way through the morass of disruptions heading their way, successful business leaders may be able to provide considerable encouragement and support to community college presidents.
- On the other hand, the community college may at times move ahead more rapidly in learning how to integrate the technologies and will be of tremendous assistance and support to the business community.
- The ride may be rough at times, but the creative and innovative thinking, both within the college and within the business

- community, can assist each other in getting successfully through the dangerous pathways.
- Nanotechnology most likely will not reach stage two before 2040–2045.
- Nanotechnology is a method of constructing things, not using plastic, steel, wood, concrete, fiberglass, or any combination of them. Rather, it uses atoms to construct products.
- Working in the quantum world with atoms, nanotechnology operates where the laws developed by Isaac Newton do not exist.
- Quantum physics has discovered that atoms exist in two or more places at the same time.
- The quantum world of atoms and molecules is not an easy or safe place to work.
- Nanotechnology is in stage one developing at a fairly slow pace.
- In the quantum world, operational nanotechnology would be able to create anything out of atoms.
- Nanotechnology could be a world-changer.
- Just because it is difficult to envision, does not mean that community colleges will not be involved in training and education of employees working in the nanotechnology arena.
- Artificial intelligence technology (AI) is already prominent in the world today. Some obvious examples are Siri and Alexa, which are known as narrow AI.
- As long as artificial technology remains narrow and specific, it will do much to enhance the lives of human beings.
- There is no end to the way narrow AI can assist and support life on the planet.
- A computer and/or robot with a mind like a human with an IQ of 600 or so is a bit frightening to say the least.
- The computer mind of AGI or ASI is called a singularity. How close is that kind of being?
- Narrow artificial technology, which exists today in many forms, could according to futurist Ray Kurtzweil, has the potential to morph into artificial general intelligence by 2030 using the power of quantum computing.
- It is quite obvious that artificial intelligence will soon contain computer power that could be used for the great benefit of mankind or the possible demise of the human race.

The Big Three Technologies

- The leaders in community colleges will need to know what is coming, when it is coming, how to plan for it, and what actions to take.
- It will all depend on whether AGI/ASI are able to be controlled by humankind.
- If two elephants in the room are not enough, the third is quantum computing.
- In September 2019, Google announced that it had successfully developed an operational quantum computer.
- The Chinese are investing $10 billion in a 4 million square foot facility that will deal only with quantum metrology and quantum computing.
- As long as quantum computing only speeds up various business, educational, health, government, and military processes, the community college will find many opportunities for training in the high velocity method of developing procedures, following up on them, and creating new ways to benefit mankind.
- The three big elephants in the room as described in this chapter coexist with the seven twenty-first-century technologies discussed in chapter 4.
- Amazon, Uber, and Airbnb give inklings of the speed and wide spectrum of change can happen when that second stage is in effect.

Chapter 6

Revisions

The community college in the twenty-first century will run head on into a variety of disruptions caused by the ten technologies that are being developed and will arrive at stage two in the near future. At the moment, in the early 2020s, there is still time to consider which of them will affect a specific college, as some institutions will be impacted with more of the technologies than others. A community college located in a large metropolitan area has the potential of being impacted by all ten of the technologies, while smaller institutions residing in rural areas may only be directly affected by a few of them.

WHICH TECHNOLOGIES COME FIRST?

Technologies such as 3D printing, autonomous vehicles, and the internet of things most likely will affect all community colleges to some degree. They are relatively reasonable to adapt to with individual courses, certificates and in some cases, associate degrees. Faculty to teach the courses and develop the curricula could probably be found in the college already. Some faculty may need further training, new equipment may be needed and, perhaps in some cases, new facilities will need to be constructed, each of which will bring added costs the institution. However, those three are most likely the easiest technologies to deal with.

ADDITIVE MANUFACTURED HOUSING

However, each of the technologies may lead to unforeseen disruptions, if the leadership of the college does not fully understand that the new technologies may morph into areas not planned for, such as additive manufacturing. House construction using the 3D method of creating a product through the use of multiple layers is currently at its beginning stages in the United States. The benefits of constructing an additive manufactured house are many, including a price point far below normal stick build homes, rapid construction of the exterior walls and roofs that can withstand low category hurricane winds.

FOREIGN DEVELOPMENT

Many European countries and the United States are seriously experimenting with the possibilities in the prototype stage, normal work behind the scenes with very little fanfare. On the other hand, two countries have moved ahead with this kind of construction, China and Mexico. China has developed single family homes and multistory office buildings, which demonstrate the benefit of price point, rapid construction, and buildings that can withstand harsh weather conditions. Mexico has developed entire subdivisions of additive manufactured homes for low income families.

MOVING TO STAGE TWO

These three technologies are expected to move to stage two, the exponential stage, within the next five to ten years, as is indicated on the chart in chapter 4 of this book. That should allow sufficient time for the research, planning, preparation, and fund-raising needed for the impacted community colleges to adapt to the workforce needs they will bring. Presidents will need to be ready to lead their institutions successfully as the technologies reach stage two and create changes in the business community, which in turn, will require training for new workforce members and retraining for existing the existing workers.

FUNDING RESOURCES

Dealing successfully with the development of what is needed can be accomplished with careful long-range planning of needs for faculty, facilities, equipment and more. Funding for these needs could be obtained through grants that may be available at the federal level, through funding from the general assembly, from donations from local businesses which need employees to work in those areas, and through the work of the foundation of the institution using fund-raising campaigns. Whatever the funding sources, the leadership of the community college will need to have the changes planned out and requests for additional funding formulated. These three technologies are relatively easy to incorporate into the institution.

QUANTUM COMPUTING

There is one technology, quantum computing, one of the big elephants in the room in the world of computing, that is a real game-changer. It is expected to reach stage two by the late 2020s/early 2030s. This technology is one to watch and research its development very carefully. There is the possibility that quantum computing will so increase the computing speed and data storage that it will be possible to create a computer mind equal to that of a human being by 2030 with an IQ of 600: artificial general intelligence. Following that mentality level, with quantum computing, the possibility of an artificial super intelligence with an IQ in the millions could be developed within another year or less.

Perhaps the development of AGI will take longer, perhaps all countries in the world will agree not to develop the AGI, or perhaps the AGI will be fully controlled when it is created. Whatever the case, this is a technology to be continually researched to learn what is developing and how the process is being controlled. Making the assumption that the AGI will be developed and fully controlled, community college leadership will need to understand how it will affect the business community and what the workforce needs will be. This is not a technology to ignore or take little interest in; it is a true game changer in the computer world, and it will require revisions on at the community college level.

REVISIONS REQUIRED

As it moves into stage two, quantum computing could require revisions in business, health, and technical programs. The business community will be extensively impacted by the rapidity that quantum computing brings. Decisions will have to be made in a matter of days rather than weeks. Processes may be developed with greatly increased speed. Workers will need to be prepared for life in the fast zone. Community colleges will need to train and educate the workforce to successfully deal with the increase in speed and decision-making at all levels.

The health field will see rapidly increased diagnosis, prescriptions and procedures developed both within the medical center and externally with doctors, pharmacies, medical production companies. As things change exceedingly more rapidly, health programs may be pushed to increase the speed at which the training of students preparing for entry into health programs takes place. Programs in nursing, dental hygiene, surgical assisting, and a number of others will need to be redesigned to meet the needs of the health employers.

Quantum computing may also create changes in the associate of arts and associate of science programs. Students taking liberal arts and science courses will need to understand the impact of this extremely high-speed computing. It will improve research considerably and impact learning on all levels including composition, humanities, science, and a host of other courses now taught from a historical perspective. All programs will need a growth mentality to be able to successfully deal with the multitude of changes that will arise from computing using atoms.

Community college leaders will have to work diligently to keep up with what will be needed and make plans to incorporate them. If the technology hits stage two that will impact the college arrives and the college is not ready, it could be disastrous. Continual research into the development of technologies, planning extensively on how to incorporate into the learning process and taking action to meet the changes when they arrive is extremely important to the success of the institution. It will be important to keep the development of Amazon, Uber, and Airbnb in mind, and in terms of quantum computing, understand the predictions of Ray Kurtzweil.

BITCOIN/BLOCKCHAIN

Bitcoin/Blockchain has the potential of completely changing the financial area internationally. In fact, underdeveloped countries may accept it sooner than developed countries because it offers a monetary system that does not use banks or money supported by a particular country. The bank of cryptocurrency is basically numbers on a spreadsheet. It is truly a digital system that, if it works properly, creates its own accounting system without the use of traditional banks or a country-supported financial system such as dollars, pounds, yens, or any other system currently used globally. The use of cryptocurrency is determined by the users and the transactions are handled by computer algorithms.

Impact on the Community College

To a community college this could mean that the payment of tuition and fees, allocations from the general assembly, and the donations provided by individuals, businesses, or other organizations could be completed by Bitcoin. That is a significance change in how college funding and budgets currently operate. It would also affect program offerings in business and accounting, which would have to be revised considerably. It might also mean developing entirely new program offerings that would be totally cryptocurrency based. Add quantum computing to the mix and change not only would happen, but it would develop extremely rapidly.

When could Bitcoin/Blockchain type currencies move to stage two? Expectations are for the early 2030s, if the issues facing crypto-currency can be resolved. In the United States, if the federal government moved to the use of some kind a digital currency, the fallout could happen nationally in a very short time. Again, it is a technology to keep track of as it develops. If successful it would directly affect the financial division of the college and the training divisions. Undoubtedly, Associate of Arts and Sciences programs would be impacted as well. It is a technology that could affect the community college on a wide spectrum of disciplines.

GENOME DEVELOPMENT

Genome development, medical and agriculture, is expected to develop and impact community college in the early 2030s. Medical genome development will affect a wider variety of current health programs as well as generate the need for a program specifically in the genome area. Programs such as nursing, dental hygiene, medical laboratory technology, physical therapist assistant, radiology, respiratory therapy, and surgical technology will be affected, some considerably, others to a lesser degree. The college will need to be prepared for the changes.

Medical genome development is expected to move to stage two in the early 2030s. It will require updating and retraining of faculty, new equipment to serve the instruction, and in some cases, additional facilities. All of these changes within the college will require additional funding. College leadership will need to obtain the needed funds through federal grants, allocations from the general assembly, fund-raising campaigns, and the like. The disruptions caused by the technologies will create continual issues and require considerable efforts by the leaders in the community college.

AGRICULTURAL PROGRAMS

For community colleges offering agricultural programs, the agricultural genome development has the potential for numerous changes in courses ranging from growing crops to breeding and feeding livestock. Additional funding will be needed to support the training and updating of faculty, new equipment, and possibly, facilities. There may seem to be no end to the apparent continuing cycle of changes that the stage two exponential level will bring. Community college administrators will be kept more than busy planning for the technology impacts, which unfortunately, will follow one upon the other.

PERSONAL ROBOTS

As has been previously mentioned, almost behind the scenes there is the development of personal robots. Japan, China, South Korea, the

United States, and some European countries have been working on personal robots for a number of years. Personal robots that can walk, jump, talk, mentally grow through experience, and look very much like human beings are expected to reach stage two in the mid-2030s. Within the next decade, personal robots will be working the community college campus, doing a number of tasks currently being completed by human beings.

Personal Robots at the Community College

Expect to see robots mowing the lawns, serving as security day and night, meeting students and visitors at the receptionist desk, cleaning hallways, classrooms and labs, delivering on campus mail, and the like. These robots will have a human look, provide much needed tasks, and will not tire or become sick. In addition, they will cost less than humans doing the same jobs, which will help to keep the college budget within the resources available. It may seem extreme today, but robots could also assist faculty in the classroom and in the long run may even replace faculty members in certain programs offered at the college.

New Programs

Not only will personal robots provide work at the college, they will also create the need for program offerings in robot repair and maintenance, robot work algorithms, and courses and programs not envisioned yet. The point is that when personal robots move to stage two, they would soon be everywhere working, assisting, and providing many tasks that were once the domain of human beings.

NANOTECHNOLOGY

Finally, a word about nanotechnology, which is expected to move to stage two in the mid-2040s. The ability to construct anything out of atoms is another phenomenal game changer as it could push 3D printing into the corner dust heap. The potential is as broad as the imagination. One thing that really stands out is the possibility that any country in the world that could obtain the facilities, equipment, and trained workforce could literally make anything that it could turn around and market the product on the world market.

The big question is, how would it affect the community college? Certainly, the process would need a trained workforce resulting in a new program offering or perhaps a number of them. It is hard to say at this point in time because what will be needed is not known in any great detail. Perhaps the college could create its own equipment if the technology could be developed on the campus. At the moment that possibility seems far-fetched because of the working environment needed for success in the quantum environment. However, given time, that issue may be overcome.

Since nanotechnology works at the atom level, and atoms apparently exist throughout the universe, it might be possible in the future to travel to other planets in our solar system or the entire galaxy and create what would be needed to live on another planet by using nanotechnology. One other possibility, although there is no current published thinking or evidence that it could be done, if most anything could be made from atoms, how about a human being? That may seem like a bridge too far, but what if?

CONCLUSION

It is clear to see that revisions in the community college environment will be many and continuous as the twenty-first century moves along. It will take foresight, research, discussion and careful planning on the part of the leadership of the community college to keep it not only afloat, but a useful educational system for the student, the business community, and local economic development.

CHAPTER 6 SUMMARY

- The community college in the twenty-first century will run head on into a variety of disruptions caused by the ten technologies that are being developed and will arrive at stage two in the near future.

- Certain technologies such as 3D printing, autonomous vehicles, and the Internet of Things most likely will affect all community colleges to some degree.
- Whatever the funding source, the leadership of the community college will need to have the changes planned out and requests for additional funding made.
- However, each of the technologies may lead to unforeseen disruptions, if the leadership of the college does not fully understand that the new technologies may morph into areas not planned for, such as additive manufacturing.
- Two countries have moved ahead with additive manufacturing construction, China and Mexico.
- These three technologies are expected to move to stage two, the exponential stage, within the next five to ten years, as is indicated on the chart in chapter 4 of this book.
- There is the possibility that quantum computing will so increase the computing speed and data storage that it will be possible to create a computer mind with an IQ of 600 by 2030, artificial general intelligence.
- Perhaps the development of AGI will take longer, perhaps all countries in the world will agree not to develop the AGI, or perhaps the AGI will be fully controlled when it is created.
- Obviously, quantum computing could require revisions in business, health, and technical programs. It may also create changes in the associate of arts and associate of science programs.
- Bitcoin/Blockchain has the potential of completely changing the financial area internationally.
- To a community college, this could mean that the payment of tuition and fees, allocations from the general assembly, and the donations provided by individuals, companies, or other organizations could be completed by Bitcoin for example.
- This is a technology to keep track of as it develops.
- Medical genome development will affect a wider variety of current health programs as well as generate the need for a program specifically in the genome area.
- All of these changes within the college will require additional funding through federal grants, allocations from the general assembly, fund-raising campaigns and the like.

- For some community colleges, those offering agricultural programs, the agricultural genome development has the potential for numerous changes in courses ranging from growing crops to breeding and feeding livestock.
- Within the next decade, personal robots will be working the community college campus doing a number of tasks currently being completed by human beings.
- Not only will personal robots provide work at the college, they will also create the need for program offerings in robot repair and maintenance, robot work algorithms, and probably courses and programs not envisioned yet.
- The ability to construct anything out of atoms is another phenomenal game changer as it could push 3D printing into corner dust heap. The potential of as broad as the imagination.
- Since nanotechnology works at the atom level, and since atoms apparently exist throughout the universe, it might be possible in the future not only to travel to other planets in our solar system or the entire galaxy, but create what would be needed to live on another planet using nanotechnology.
- It will take foresight, research, discussion, and careful thinking on the part of the leadership of the community college to keep it not only afloat, but a useful educational system for the student, the business community and local economic development.

Chapter 7

Securing the Future

Those in community college leadership in the twenty-first century can learn a great deal from those leading business alongside of them. CEOs of businesses are being coached by researchers who understand that the current century is developing differently than the former one. As Buckminster Fuller stated that "there is one outstanding important fact regarding Spaceship Earth, and that is that no instruction book came with it" (Fuller, 1969, p. 52). That simple statement written over fifty years ago rings true today. The instruction manual is being developed as time goes by; it upgrades continuously. The other important component needed to understand about this century is, "Don't prepare for change, prepare for acceleration" (Gutsche, 2020, p. 98).

SUPPORT FOR THE BUSINESS COMMUNITY

Business leaders have been receiving considerable amounts of information and directions for success in the twenty-first century for many years already. Jeff Bezos developed Amazon based on what he heard, read, and experienced. He stated, "Long term thinking levers our existing attitudes and lets us do new things we couldn't otherwise contemplate" (Bezos, 2021, p. 84). Undoubtedly business leaders have always looked the future, at least the very near future, to create their plans. They got used to doing planning using a "present-forward" method, which led to short term thinking based in what is going on in the present (Johnson et al., 2020, p. 8).

Using that kind of planning did not allow those in leadership to see what was farther out in the future that might directly impact their business. In the past century, if something unforeseen arrived, the business could make modifications to their planning and subsequent operation. In the current century, to be blind to what will disrupt the business with exponential, accelerating velocity may create disaster for the business. Johnson (2020) recommends future-back thinking in which the business would look far into the future to determine trends and possibilities that may occur and create plans to deal with the disruptions before they occur.

FUTURE-BACK PLANNING

Future-back planning will require continuous research into what might happen and what could impact the business. Further, the process would develop a vision of what the future will look like for the business and then create plans to work successfully toward it. "Creating a vision, translating it into a future-back strategy, and then programming and implementing it is not a discrete event within a corporation's life. In a way, it *is* its life" (Johnson et al., 2020. p. 138). Success will require a dynamic vision followed by dynamic strategic planning. In other words, those leaders who understand and integrate an ever-changing vision and planning process will be the ones leading successful businesses.

Successful business CEOs will be those who took the time to learn how success is created in this century. It is quite different from the skills used in the previous century. It will take continuous research into what is coming that can affect the business, when it will disrupt current practices, and, most importantly, how to deal with the potential upset before it happens. It will take continuous planning and actions to keep up with the changes in order to and stay ahead of the competition to secure the future of the business. The twenty-first century will require a set of requirements for success that will need to be identified and taught in leadership programs at the university level.

TEACHING METHODS IN THE TWENTY-FIRST CENTURY

Community colleges are in many ways like a business. They obtain revenue, hire faculty and staff, and develop an education product—a graduate, who goes out into the business world with the skills required for a successful career. How can the community college faculty best teach what needs to be understood by the students who desire successful careers in the twenty-first century? According to Thomas Bailey et al., (2015), "Researchers have identified two distinct approaches to college teaching, known as *knowledge transmission* and *learning facilitation*" (p. 85). These are two very different approaches to the teaching/learning process in higher education.

KNOWLEDGE TRANSMISSION

"Faculty who adhere to the knowledge transmission model tend to focus on facts rather than concepts, cover a large amount of content in class, and emphasize lectures, readings, and other use of media to impart information" (Bailey et al., p. 85). This is the traditional method of teaching using the faculty member lecturing in front of the class, while the students are taking notes. Those notes and a textbook together present the information needed for the student who will be required to recall it on tests given later in the course. This method will not work well in an environment that is continuously changing in real time. The time of the "sage on the stage" will disappear. The "guide on the side" will become the new normal.

LEARNING FACILITATION

Twenty-first century education must change to student-focused learning or what is known as learning facilitation:

> Faculty members who adhere to the learning facilitation model are explicitly focused on how to motivate students and help them "to learn how to learn." They tend to use more collaborative, discussion-based, and activity-based teaching methods, and assess student performance through

discussions, writing assignments and projects that emphasize critical thinking. (Bailey et al., 2015, p. 87)

The use of the learning facilitation will need to become the primary method in the classroom and lab in order for the student to learn in an accelerative business community. The ten technologies discussed earlier in the book, and other technologies to follow, demand that those in the workforce be ready and willing to learn what is needed in a rapid, continual manner. Student-focused learning will provide the student with the ability and attitude needed for staying current with the changes in the business to keep it current with the accelerating use of various technologies.

MAGIC BULLET

Learning facilitation is as close to a magic bullet as the educational world has ever used. It will help to make the student a real, continuous learner as opposed to a regurgitator of facts and information for a specific time frame. After graduation he or she will be able to understand not only what the current situation with a particular job is, but also what it will change to in the near and distant future. Those changes and more to follow will be understood and expected by the members of the workforce. Those changes will keep the business competitive with the workforce knowing how important their ability to upgrade is to the health of the organization.

DEVELOPING A WORKFORCE FOR THE TWENTY-FIRST CENTURY

The business community already knows it faces ever-accelerating changes caused by technologies that exist and those that will appear in the future. It needs a workforce that accepts the dynamic workplace and the ability to adapt to it. That is why community college faculty will need to alter their methods of instruction to the learning facilitation model. Faculty develop courses that put them in the position of the learning manager with the students taking on the serious business of learning how to learn. There are methods that can be used to assist in the change from the sage on the stage to the guide on the side as will be discussed in chapter 8.

CONCLUSION

As was noted at the beginning of this chapter, both business CEOs and community college presidents have much that could be learned together when becoming successful in a dynamic, accelerating world of change that both business and education will face. Ideas and methods that work in one arena may work well in the other with some alteration. It will be up to leaders in both the business and educational world to work together in learning the parameters of success in the technology driven twenty-first century. Since both areas are going be disrupted by some, if not many, of the ten developing technologies, how to deal successfully with stage two will be advantageous to all.

CHAPTER 7 SUMMARY

- CEOs of businesses are being coached by researchers who understand that the current century is developing differently than the former one.
- Business leaders have been receiving considerable amounts of information and directions for success in the twenty-first century for many years already.
- In the current century, to be blind to what will disrupt the business with exponential, accelerating velocity may create disaster for the business.
- The future-back planning process will require continuous research into what might happen and what could impact the business.
- Community college faculty must determine how to best teach what needs to be understood by the students who desire successful careers in the twenty-first century.
- According to Thomas Bailey et al, (2015), "Researchers have identified two distinct approaches to college teaching, known as *knowledge transmission* and *learning facilitation*" (p. 85).

- The use of learning facilitation, the student-focused model will need to become the primary method in the classroom and lab in order for the student to learn in an accelerative business community.
- Student-focused learning will provide the student with the ability and attitude needed for staying current with the changes in the business to keep it current with the accelerating use of various technologies.
- After graduation, he or she will be able to understand not only what the current situation with a particular job is, but also what it will move to into in the near and distant future.
- The business community already knows it faces ever-accelerating changes caused by technologies that exist and those that will appear in the future.
- It needs a workforce that accepts the dynamic workplace and the ability to adapt to it.
- It will be up to leaders in both the business and educational world to work together in learning the parameters of success in the technology driven twenty-first century.

Chapter 8

Students

The central focal point of community colleges is the students. They are the reason that community colleges exist. Administration, faculty, and staff are needed for successful college operation. Administrators make sure the funding is appropriate to the needs for the educational process, facilities, and equipment to serve the students. Faculty provide the classroom and lab instruction. Staff provide recruitment, counseling, advising, library services, and financial operation, all of which together ultimately serve the student by creating a viable learning environment.

WHAT STUDENTS PROVIDE

For the benefit of the college, students provide revenue through their tuition and fees paid each semester. The percentage of what that revenue covers in terms of the budget is in the 20–35% range of the total revenue. Second, student numbers in terms of full-time equivalent enrollment (FTEs) provide funding from the state covering somewhere in the 50–75% range of the revenue. The remainder comes from local sources, alternative sources, grants, and donations. Without students, the mission of the community college and two serious segments of its revenue disappear, and the institution would cease to be.

WHAT GRADUATES PROVIDE

For the benefit of the graduates are the jobs they assume that provide financial security for themselves and their families. Graduates may go on for further academic or professional education, which in turn makes them more valuable in the workplace, more able to obtain leadership positions, and more willing to support others in the community who may be less fortunate than they are. "It is clear that some leaders, more than others, demonstrate a persistent, almost zealous drive to ensure student success while at the same time maintaining access for the broad range of students community colleges have traditional served" (Crisis and Opportunity, 2013, p. 5).

For the benefit of the community, graduates become successful members of the local workforce and through their work in various local organizations. They help raise the economic value of the community and increase the living standards of the region. Many end up leading businesses, some venture into elective office, others support their churches, and most raise families who understand the value of higher education. Further, college administrators and faculty work in the community on various boards and committees for the betterment of all concerned.

THE COMMUNITY COLLEGE MOVEMENT

Historically, the original idea for a junior college, generated by William Rainey Harper as president of the University of Chicago, was for an internal college at the university that would improve the student's ability to complete a bachelor's degree at the university. Over the years, from that beginning junior colleges spread all over the United States, which by the 1960s became community colleges. The development of the two-year college allowed millions of individuals to make a life for themselves and their families that was far beyond anything their ancestors had envisioned. The notion that almost anyone who was interested could have the opportunity to access a higher education benefitted millions of students.

GENERATION-Z STUDENTS

That focus on the student has not changed in the twenty-first century. In fact, it is more important than ever today. The next generation of students, Gen Z, is here now and ready to learn how to deal with the technological changes created by the ten technologies and others that may appear. Since the changes are likely to come rapidly, creating disruptions, with one following the other over a five to twenty-year timeframe, it will require new skills to be learned, which in turn will be modified continuously. Gen Z students are already accustomed to rapid changes in the world of technology in which they have grown up. They are already somewhat prepared for the impact that the ten technologies will have on business, heath, education, and life in general.

LEARNING HOW TO LEARN

The technological world of the current century will demand that the members of the workforce are open to change, willing to acquire new skills rapidly, and understand that the work-world changes exponentially just as the technologies do. It will be critical that students *learn how to learn*, at first in a school environment, but later in their work careers, on their own. The repetitive job of the twentieth century will be replaced by the ever-changing jobs of the twenty-first. To deal with that kind of workforce environment will demand a student-focused style of learning that is discussed in chapter 9.

CHALLENGES FOR LEADERSHIP

"Given the rapidly changing environment in which community colleges operate, presidents in the future will almost certainly confront different challenges than those facing presidents in the past" (Crisis and Opportunity, 2013, p.9). The current century will place demands on those in the workforce much different from anything experienced in the past. Students must be prepared for what is to come.

Community colleges will have to revise and reconstruct the learning methods used in every department and discipline. The methods of instruction that worked well in the past will only provide obstacles to the learning needed in the near future. There is still some time to research and investigate what changes are needed; however, community colleges which do not take action soon will find themselves in trouble as the world changes around them without asking their permission.

PREPARING THE STUDENT FOR SUCCESS

Current researchers are providing hints and possibilities of what the student has to learn to live successfully through the coming decades. In *Stretch: How to Future-Proof Yourself for Tomorrow's Workplace,* Willyerd and Mistick (2016) argue that "Preparing for a career tomorrow means anticipating what the future will look like and what capabilities will be needed" (p. 186). The future will demand that members of the workforce will be very much on their own in determining what is affecting their current positions and, more importantly, what they will have to do as a result.

The ability to make such determinations and decide what actions to take will rest with the individual. The ability to *learn how learn* will be of the greatest benefit to the individual and ultimately to the success of the business which employs them. All of which will lead to a kind of entrepreneurial attitude on the part of the members of the workforce. "The valued contributor of tomorrow will adapt to any situation with creative resolve and always have the ability to revisit and modify while still engaged in a methodical problem-solving process (Willyerd et al., 2026, p. 202).

This advice demonstrates the need for the graduate to become a valued member of the workforce is to always be looking ahead, determining what is coming, and deciding what action to take for. All this is possible for the individual who has adequately learned how to learn. It will be a continuous, ongoing process that may at times be fully as stressful as the job the individual is holding. Further, it puts pressure on the community college to instill in the students how critically important it is to become a learner. It makes student-focused learning the method to be used for the student's benefit.

CAPABILITIES NEEDED

Members of the twenty-first century workforce are expected to need cognitive abilities, system skills, complex problem-solving capabilities, content skills, process skills, social skills, resource management skills, and technical skills (Schwab, 2018). Those needed the most are the first three listed. Those needed least are the last two named. Note how the first three all have to do with mind and the last one with the hands. Klaus Schwab is the founder and executive chairman of the World Economic Forum. His interest in the ten technologies and their impact on society is highlighted in his book (Schwab, 2016).

WORKING IN A DIGITAL WORLD

Schwab's book, *The Fourth Industrial Revolution* (2016), takes a serious look at what the exponential, digital world looks like, indicates what must be done to prepare for it, and cites expectations as to when various technologies will reach a tipping point. In the book he discusses the smartphone, the cloud, the internet of things, the smart home, smart cities, autonomous cars, artificial intelligence, robots, cryptocurrency, 3D printing and additive manufacturing, designer beings, and more (Schwab, 2016). Some, if not all of these items, will affect the students of community colleges after they graduate and join the world of work.

Schwab sees tipping points for each of the technologies that take place at about the time, some before and others after, that each of them is expected to reach stage two. The differences in timing are close enough to be of no statistical significance. The importance is that community college students in the 2020s and 2030s will experience almost all them in their explosive stage of development. Schwab's tipping predictions parallel the expectations of stage two, which those in business, health, and education will experience. Both provide support for the student-focused learning model.

LEARNING SUCCESS

On one hand it is clear that creating an instructional milieu that can produce graduates who have the tools to become successful in the world of work is an excellent idea. On the other hand, that type of instructional environment can only become a reality when community college leaders and faculty understand what is coming with the ten technologies and adapt their teaching methods to help students become successful in both the school and workplace environments.

The student remains the key focus of the community college. Administrators will need to lead the faculty toward student-focused learning. This may take serious revisions of current teaching methods. To make the change to student-focused learning, training will be needed to help the faculty make appropriate changes on how learning takes place. It will cost the college funding to make the adaptation; it will take planning and decision-making by the college leadership. When the leadership of the institution and the faculty work together to make the shift to a student-focused learning method, students can expect to find themselves in a learning environment conducive to the ever-changing needs of the business community and success in their individual careers.

LEARNING METHODS

Student-focused learning methods that help the student learn how to learn already exist. They include the flipped classroom, concept-based instruction, gaming, project-based instruction, virtual reality instruction, MOOC, and online instruction, as well as instructional methods created by YouTube and Google. It may be difficult for some faculty members to make the shift from the lecture/discussion method of teaching to student-focused methods, but the shift will make all the difference in the learning on the part of students in the twenty-first century and graduates who move into a technology dominated work world.

CONCLUSION

Students first, a concept easy to agree with, but more of a challenge to fulfill in the current century when merely knowing the facts is not enough. Learning how to learn in a rapidly changing work environment will take serious changes in how faculty and students interact in the classroom and lab.

CHAPTER 8 SUMMARY

- The central focal point of community colleges is the students.

- For the benefit of the college, students provide revenue through their tuition and fees paid each semester.
- For the benefit of the graduates are jobs they assume that provide for them and their families financially.
- They [graduates] help raise the economic value of the community and increase the living standards of the region.
- The notion that almost anyone who was interested could have the opportunity to access a higher education benefitted millions of students.
- Gen Z students are already accustomed to rapid change in the world of technology in which they have grown up.
- It will be critical that students *learn how to learn*, at first in a school environment, but later in their work careers, on their own.
- The current century will place demands on those in the workforce much different from anything experienced in the past.
- The methods of instruction that worked well in the past will only provide obstacles to the learning needed in the near future.
- The future will demand that members of the workforce will be very much on their own in determining what is affecting their current positions and, more importantly, what they will have to do as a result.
- The ability to *learn how learn* will be of the greatest benefit to the individual and ultimately to the success of the business which employs them.
- Members of the twenty-first century workforce are expected to need cognitive abilities, system skills, complex problem-solving capabilities, content skills, process skills, social skills, resource management skills, and technical skills (Schwab, 2018).
- Schwab sees tipping points for each of the technologies that take place at about the time, some before and others after, of the expectation that each of them reaches stage two.
- To make the change to student-focused learning, training will be needed to help the faculty make appropriate changes on how learning takes place.
- It may be difficult for some faculty members to make the shift from the lecture/discussion method of teaching to student-focused methods, but the shift will make all the difference in the learning

on the part of students in the twenty-first century and graduates who move into a technology-dominated work world.

Chapter 9

Learning Methods

There already exist a number of student-focused, learning facilitation methods that, depending on the program or discipline, can be reviewed and adopted. They are described and discussed in greater detail using the perspective of specific program offerings or situations in the book *Student-Focused Learning: Higher Education in an Exponential Digital Era* (Staat, 2020). The following will give a brief overview of nine methods. The future will undoubtedly see more possibilities.

IMPACTS ON THE FACULTY

In general, moving to a student-focused learning method of education requires a good deal of change on the part of the faculty member and the student. The faculty member has to learn to use a teaching methodology he or she may not be familiar with. The traditional teaching method of lecture-discussion with the teacher in the position of the sage on the stage is replaced with the faculty member as a learning manager or the guide on the side. The change means that a teaching method that has worked in the past will need to be replaced with one that is based in the notion of learning how to learn, which means a revision and overhaul of the lecture/discussion method commonly used for decades.

IMPACTS ON THE STUDENT

The impact on the teacher is one part of the equation; the other is what is changed for the student. As will be seen in the methods described below, the student will take on much more of the learning process when learning how to learn. The changes are necessary for both the faculty member and the student because of the accelerating changes that will take place in the twenty-first-century business community, medical field, and technical workplace. In order for the graduate to be successful in the digital world of work, the graduate will be hired in a workplace that changes continuously, making constant upgrading of each member of the workforce a necessity. It is that dynamic workplace that will require that learning be an ongoing process throughout one's career.

LEARNING TO LEARN

Students will need to understand how the digital world of work operates. They will need to learn how to make upgrading themselves to the latest developments in the business environment an ongoing process. Learning how to learn by and for themselves will become critical to success. As a result, although learning to become a successful automotive technician, a nurse, business manager, dental hygienist, welder, electronics technician or any other trade or profession is begun at the community college, that is only the beginning. The ten technologies, plus more in the offing, are changing diametrically what it meant to learn in the past and what it will mean to learn for the future.

STUDENT-FOCUSED METHODS

What the graduate will need for success in the future world of work is the ability to learn on their own. The best methods to assist them in learning how to learn are already in existence; all of them are student-focused learning methods, which place the student directly into self-learning rather than learning through the traditional lecture/discussion method. A number of methods that can be used are described below.

ONLINE AND MASSIVE OPEN ONLINE COURSES (MOOC)

There are two harbingers of student-focused learning: online education and MOOC education. By default, these two methods have already placed a great deal of emphasis of *learning how to learn* on the student. Online education received a tremendous boost in 2020 because of the COVID-19 pandemic. Educators and students on all levels had to learn overnight how to use Zoom or some other online delivery method as of March of that year. When instruction switched from face-to-face to online teaching, a significant burden to learn was placed on the student.

In addition, many faculty members had to learn how to effectively use a teaching modality they had little or no experience with. This obviously created serious issues that had to be resolved in the shortest time possible. For some the metaphor of flying the airplane while building it was exactly how they felt. The MOOCs, which may be modified somewhat in character as time goes by, remain as a teaching method. Both online and MOOC methods of teaching bring student-focused learning to the forefront.

THE FLIPPED CLASSROOM

A third method is the flipped classroom. Lectures by the instructor are videoed by the instructor and made available to the students before entering the classroom. Students come to class with a background learned before the class session and use the session to clarify issues or practice *hands-on* procedures. This method has been already successfully used to some degree in high school, undergraduate, and graduate courses. Instructors who have successfully used the flipped classroom approach make some suggestions to faculty who are interested in implementing the method.

Suggestions for Success. The instructor should first determine whether the course being offered could successfully use the flipped classroom. Courses in biology, chemistry, physics, welding, machine tool, automotive, nursing, health programs and many others which have a hands-on component(s) in the course will find use of the flipped classroom very helpful. Second, when beginning to use the flipped classroom, the instructor should start with just one segment of course to see how it works. After success with a particular segment, they can move on to others. For best results, the instructor should not try starting the method with everything in the course all at once.

Work in Partnership. Third, if possible, work with another faculty member as a partner in the development and implementation of the course. Many instructors make videos explaining what they had normally lectured on in class. Students watch those at home and come to class ready to apply the learning through hands on projects or in class discussions. Fourth, faculty who use this method have found that it must be explained carefully to the students in advance so that they understand why it is being done and how the students will benefit from them. This process places the focus of the learning on the student, which helps the student learn how to learn on their own, so critical to their success in their future careers in a rapidly changing technological world (Bergman et al., 2021).

CONCEPT-BASED EDUCATION

A fourth student-focused learning method is concept-based education. The instructor discusses broad concepts that underlie the basic concepts of the course. The students investigate various perspectives on the basics and come to class prepared to present what they have learned and discuss how they support the basic concepts previously presented. This method is often used in health programs where the facts are important, but the concepts are equally as critical to understand. The instructor can also use the classroom to initiate new concepts and ask the students to research the facts that support the concepts.

Guided Questions and Case Studies. Another approach is for the instructor to ask guiding questions for the students to research and come back to class providing the information they have discovered and discuss the various factual information that leads to appropriate responses to the original guiding question posed by the instructor. Case studies can be used that provide concepts which the student has to solve through research and come to class prepared to present the research and discuss appropriate answers to the issues involved.

The purpose for using concept-based instruction is to move the instructor to the position of learning manager and guide and to help the students to learn how to learn, using facts, research, and real-life situations which will prepare them to be job ready.

PROJECT-BASED EDUCATION

A fifth student-focused method is project-based education, a student-driven, instructor-facilitated approach to learning (Bell, 2010). The method provides the student with opportunities to choose a subject that is approved by the instructor. The aim is to use an issue that students can pursue within the parameters of the course. As an example, it could begin with a question or issue of local or national concern. The topic will ask students to study a challenging problem requiring him or her to engage in research to find possible answers to the topic, reflect on the process, critique, and revise the work, and create a final product.

Student-Managed Learning. The idea behind this method is to help students to manage their learning. The project should be grounded in the real-world situations, challenges, or problems. As examples, a student in an automotive curriculum might decide to investigate the impact of autonomous cars. A student in a health program might research the potential of genome development in medical world. A student studying history might look into the impact of robots on the human workforce. There is no end to possibilities.

Students are attracted to this type of instruction because it allows them to learn about topics within the curriculum that are of interest to them. Project-based education becomes student-focused, instructor-guided, on topics of interest to the student within the subject matter of the course involved. It helps the student learn how to learn, which ultimately, is the major purpose of the method.

GAMING

The sixth method is gaming. This method also provides for student-focused learning. Game-based learning is the intentional use of digital games to fulfill a specific learning objective in a more interesting way to the student. In addition, game-based learning often provides motivation to learn on the part of the student. According to research, the use of gaming as a teaching method has positive impact on student engagement, exploration, socialization, motivation, communication, problem solving, and critical thinking skills (Wiggins, 2016).

Impact of Gaming. What is valuable when a student plays a digital game? First, continuous grading. The student has to accurately complete various tasks to continue on in the game. Second, long-term and short-term goals are clearly defined. The student knows what has to be done, but has to learn how to complete the tasks. Third, rewarding effort. The student gets credit for obtaining goals. Fourth, feedback. The student gets immediate and continuous feedback. Fifth, the element of uncertainty. The student finds surprising experiences and rewards that keeps the student from getting bored. Sixth, windows of learning. The student becomes engaged in the process and learns how to be successful. Seventh, confidence. The student learns to be confident, more willing to take risks, and harder to discourage (Ark and Wise, 2011). Students are already used to playing digital games, now all that is needed is to take gaming into the educational arena directly.

Time and Effort Needed by Faculty. The issue for faculty is not the positive result that gaming can have on student learning, it is the time and effort needed for an instructor to find and or develop the games that are useful tools for learning in the particular course being taught. Since the use of gaming is in its early stages of development in community colleges, it will take time for appropriate, successful games to be developed. The method is one that not only has tremendous potential for student learning, it may also provide pathways for creative faculty members to develop gaming courses that could be sold on the educational market.

YOUTUBE EDUCATION

A seventh student-focused method is YouTube education. Over three hundred videos are uploaded to YouTube every minute (Ace, 2016). They vary from personal interest on a variety of topics to academic presentations on a wide spectrum of subject matters. YouTube videos can be used to learn almost anything such as, solving word problems, playing an instrument, understanding historical events, hearing poetry read, and a huge variety of other topics. All instructor has to do is research what exists in the YouTube library of videos to find those that work for whatever course that is being taught.

Assistance Provided. There is assistance available to educators from YouTube. One is YouTube for educators. It provides over 500,000 educational videos from universities, PBS, Ted Talks, Khan Academy, and the like. The videos are grouped according to categories that make it easier for an instructor to search out what might work best for their particular topic of interest. Often faculty use YouTube videos as supportive information for their courses. Another assistance is the YouTube teacher, which shows the instructors how to use YouTube in the classroom. In addition, YouTube allows instructors and students to make videos that could be shown to the class.

YouTube and the Flipped Classroom. YouTube education is a natural to be combined with the flipped classroom. Assignments could be made to view certain YouTube videos as homework for students to discuss in following class sessions. YouTube education has great potential for student focused learning, once that enormous library of videos is discovered and used.

GOOGLE EDUCATION

The eighth method is Google education. Google, a technology business, has gotten extensively into the education field. Google shows teachers how to use technology to its fullest advantage. Generation Z students, who have used the latest in technology from childhood, are arriving in the classroom from kindergarten and middle school and will soon be in graduate school. They expect to continue to be student-focused learners in order to keep up with all that is going on in the world today. To help make that happen, Google for higher education has staff that partner with faculty and students in community colleges across the United States.

Development in Higher Education. They help faculty create, pilot, and test emerging technologies for the higher education classroom. Google has demonstrated both the willingness and capability to lead the digital classroom conversation. Google can assist greatly in the process of creating student-focused learning.

VIRTUAL REALITY EDUCATION

The ninth student-focused method is virtual reality education. Virtual reality has existed in various forms since the 1980s with games played with a head-mounted display that puts the student in a reality that was virtual in nature. The headset shuts out the real world for the time it is worn, and a virtual world comes into view. Today, when a student places a headset on the eyes see a three-dimensional world that is so accurate that the wearer seems to *feel* the environment just as he or she would in the real world.

The student can be transported almost anywhere in the world to see and hear what could be seen and heard as if the student were really there. "It is no accident that many of the most creative people in history have traveled more than their contemporaries, visiting faraway lands. With VR, everybody can be a world traveler, reaching the deepest corners of the universe and human imagination" (Schwab, 2018, p. 184).

VR in Athletics. The use of virtual reality is limited only by the imagination. VR has been used by university and professional football quarterbacks, who learn how to react faster to game possibilities with repeated use of the VR headsets. Further, the quarterback could work through specific plays over and over without ever getting hit or injured. On the other hand, an injured player who was out of the game for days or weeks could use the headset to replay games and learn how to increase his ability when he returns to the field (Bailenson, 2018).

VR in Curricula. VR has also been used in training students how to weld. The student dons a headset similar to that used in actual welding environment and practices welding processes similar to what he or she would do on the job. Nursing training has found uses for VR. A student can learn difficult or dangerous procedures without creating any harm to the student or the patient. Training using virtual reality is truly student-focused in almost every way possible. A simple virtual reality experience can be found using a Google cardboard headset, which costs less than $20 apiece. Or, one could use the high-end computer driven headsets like Oculus, HoloLens and HTE, which range in cost from $300–$5,000 apiece as of this writing.

CONCLUSION

In conclusion, student-focused learning will most likely become the major way students will be able to keep up with opportunities in the workforce and their careers. Faculty should prepare themselves by experimenting with the methods cited in this presentation, which will help to put them at the forefront and leadership in the digital educational world.

CHAPTER 9 SUMMARY

- There already exist a number of student-focused, learning facilitation methods which, depending on the program or discipline, could be reviewed and decided upon.
- The traditional teaching method of lecture-discussion with the teacher in the position of the sage on the stage is replaced with the faculty member as learning manager and guide on the side.
- The student will take on much more of the learning process by learning how to learn.
- Students will need to understand how the digital world of work operates.
- What the student will need as graduate for success in the future world of work is the ability to learn on their own.
- There are two harbingers of student-focused learning: online education and MOOC education.
- Instructors who have successfully used the flipped classroom approach make some suggestions to faculty who are interested in implementing the method.
- First, determining whether the course being offered could successfully use the flipped classroom.
- Second, starting with one segment of course to see how it works.
- Third, working with another faculty member as a partner in the development and implementation of the course.

- In concept-based education, the instructor discusses broad concepts that underlie the basic notions of the course.
- The students investigate various perspectives on the basics and come to class prepared to present what they have learned.
- Another approach is for the instructor to ask guiding questions for the students to research and come back to class providing the information they have discovered.
- Case studies can be used that provide concepts which the student has to solve through research and come to class prepared to present the research.
- The aim of project-based education is to use an issue that students can pursue within the parameters of the course.
- The project should be grounded in real-world situations, challenges, or problems.
- Students are attracted to this type of instruction because it allows them to learn about topics within the curriculum that are of interest to them.
- Game-based learning is the intentional use of digital games to fulfill a specific learning objective in a more interesting way to the student.
- In digital gaming, students experience continuous grading, short-term and long-term goals, rewarding effort and feedback, an element of uncertainty, windows of learning, and confidence.
- The issue for faculty is not the wonderful result that gaming can have on student learning, it is the time and effort for an instructor to develop the games that are useful tools for learning in the particular course being taught.
- YouTube videos can be used to learn almost anything, such as solving word problems, playing an instrument, understanding historical events, hearing poetry read, and a huge variety of other topics.
- There is assistance available to educators from YouTube.
- YouTube education is a natural to be combined with the flipped classroom.
- Google, a technology business, has gotten extensively involved in the education field.
- Virtual reality has been around in various forms since the 1980s with games played with a head mounted display that put the student in a reality that was virtual in nature.

- Today, when a student places a headset on, the eyes see a three-dimensional world that is so accurate that the wearer seems to *feel* the environment just as he or she would in the real world.
- VR has been used by university and professional football quarterbacks, who learn how to react faster to game possibilities with repeated use of the VR headsets.
- VR has been used in training students to weld.
- Nursing training has found uses for VR.
- Student-focused learning will most likely become the major way students will be able to keep up with opportunities in the workforce and their careers.

Chapter 10

Pathways

With ten technologies, including three potential game-changers, already in existence with more to come, presidential leadership in the community college sector is facing potential disruptions to business as usual in the near future. The exponential rise of Amazon, Uber, and Airbnb in the retail, taxi, and hotel world respectively is an indication of how rapidly technologies can develop and disrupt what was thought to be secure and normal. Those in the business world taking the technologies seriously are preparing for the onslaught as it might affect them. What then is the effect on community colleges in the twenty-first century?

QUESTIONS FOR LEADERSHIP

How does a community college president, along with administrators, faculty, staff, students, board members and those in service area of the college, react? How does the college leadership become aware, research, plan, and prepare to take successful action? What is a president to do in order to keep the college viable and useful to all stakeholders and interested parties? How does leadership itself move from what worked well in the past century to what will bring success to all concerned in the current century? What does leadership in an exponential, digital, and disruptive time look like?

GUIDING THE COMMUNITY COLLEGE: A TWO-PHASE SYSTEM

A two-phase system can be used to help guide the community college president through the potentially difficult issues the institution may face.

PHASE 1: PREPARATION

Step 1: Determining

At each community college, it will be necessary to begin by determining which of the ten technologies will have the potential to impact the college. The college president should bring together a committee of administrators, faculty, staff, business leaders, and students to discuss the technologies one at a time and decide how many of the ten will have an effect on the college and which will little or no impact. For example, if the college does not have an existing automotive program, nor expectations of starting one, that technology could be eliminated.

Artificial Intelligence and Quantum Computing. Some of the ten, such as artificial intelligence and quantum computing, will have an effect on the operation of the college no matter the size or location of the college; the question is when and to what degree? Current expectations would predict quantum computing reaching stage two by the late 2020s and artificial intelligence hitting stage two by the early 2030s. These two technologies will need to be carefully and continuously researched and monitored as they develop. They could reach stage two earlier or later than expected.

Internet of Things. Even earlier expectations are seen for the internet of things to get to stage two, about the mid-2020s, since that technology is already moving ahead rapidly using current computer power, the internet, and the cloud. Most likely most community colleges are doing little in the IoT area at the moment, but opportunities for training and education in the use of and workforce for new businesses in this area will become apparent. Autonomous vehicles could move to stage two in the late 2020s. Colleges with automotive programs will be disrupted when the autonomous cars and trucks arrive. Serious research will need to be undertaken to understand what to do when they proliferate significantly.

Other Technologies. 3D printing (additive manufacturing), Bitcoin/Blockchain, medical genome development, and agricultural genome development all have the potential to move to stage two in the early 2030s. Personal robots are expected to reach stage two in the mid-2030s. Only nanotechnology is an outlier with stage two expectations in the mid-2040s. In a nutshell, those are the stage two expectations. Any one of the technologies could move ahead faster or less rapidly than expected, which makes determining which technologies will impact a specific college an extremely important research consideration.

Step 2: Initial Internal Communication

Once a college has determined which of the technologies will most likely affect the college, that list should be communicated throughout the institution to administrators, faculty, staff, students, and board members. Transparency is critical at this point. Accurately designed presentations should be made for all concerned within the institution. Next, it is important to provide suitable time for all concerned to discuss the information and get used to the fact that serious changes face the institution. Some may find the information surprising, and others may be well aware of the situation.

Step 3: Research Committees

Appropriate internal committees should be developed to study the individual technologies which are understood to have the potential to disrupt specific areas of the college, such as the automotive department or in the case of IoT, the business department. Committees should be developed to study the development and possible impact on the college of quantum computing and artificial intelligence, because these two technologies will have an effect on all community colleges regardless of size or location. It is critical that research committees be set up in these four areas as soon as possible in order to be prepared for potential disruptions that may develop in a very short period of time.

In addition, committees should be set up to study the potential impact of 3D printing (additive manufacturing), medical genome development, and Bitcoin/Blockchain (cryptocurrency) on the college. If the college offers agriculture courses or programs, there is need for a committee on agricultural genome development. These four technologies are expected to reach stage two in the early 2030s. Again, any one of them could move faster than the expectations and college will need to be ready in case that happens.

Personal Robots and Nanotechnology. Personal robots, expected to reach stage two in the mid-2030s, and nanotechnology in the mid-2040s round out the need for two more research committees to keep them researched, monitored, and understood. Their exponential stage appears to be off into the future from the present; however, quantum computing alone could significantly increase the development of any of them. As has been pointed out previously, nanotechnology is a game-changer on a level with artificial intelligence and quantum computing. It is critical for the community college to be aware of their existence and growth.

Step 4: External Communication

Once the college has set the various committees into operation, it is important to inform the external stakeholders of what the college is doing and how it will benefit those in the business community, and potential students. The business community will need to know that the college is working internally to be knowledgeable about which technologies will have impact on the college. They will want to understand that the college is not only ready for workforce needs in the present, but is also investigating potential workforce needs in the future. Using the college website could be one valuable way to communicate to the external stakeholders.

Students will be very interested to know that the college is investigating what the future business, health, and technical fields will hold for them. They want to prepare for jobs that will exist and develop during their careers. If they see that the college is doing serious work in preparing for future employment needs, they will be more interested in enrolling in program offerings that will be of benefit to them. Students will also need advising and counseling on the coming workforce changes in order to make the best decisions. Counselors will need accurate updating on the finding of the research of the various committees.

Step 5: Periodic Internal Communication

Since the various committees are studying and researching information about a specific technology, it is important to have each committee make periodic reports. These can be done verbally in meetings with faculty and staff at the beginning and middle of each semester. If a committee is finding that a technology is closing in on stage two, more meetings may be necessary to keep all internal employees up to date on what is happening. Transparency is very important as there are some technologies that may cause serious disruptions that will affect many or all of the faculty and staff. The president will have to decide when these meetings should be held.

Communication with Faculty and Staff. Keeping the entire faculty and staff informed on the development of the technologies is critically important as some disruptions will need to be well understood, especially if they are going to impact training and educational needs of faculty and staff, create needs for additional equipment, require new or renovated facilities, and/or the possibility of modifying or deleting existing programs. The goal would be to foresee the needed changes and be able to handle them with little or no loss of faculty or staff. Careful research, periodic updating, and caring for all faculty and staff is critically important when a technology reaches stage two and impacts the institution.

PHASE 2: IMPLEMENTATION

Step 6: Retraining of Faculty and Staff

Since the development of each of the ten technologies will at some point reach stage two, with associated disruptions within the institution that directly affect some faculty and staff, the college must be prepared financially to support any retraining or reeducation needed to meet the needs required. The president must be prepared to find the sources for the financial needs that will be created by the effect the technologies may bring. It is not a matter of waiting to see what happens, it is a matter of foreseeing what may happen and being prepared for it. Disruptions can be very harmful to the concept of business as usual.

Faculty and Staff Development. Faculty will need to be developed to meet the needs for changes in existing courses, preparing new courses, and in some cases, developing an entirely new programs at the certificate or associate degree level. The normal time period of degree development and approval will most likely need to be reduced significantly in time as the business community is going to require a retrained workforce in very short order. The time frames that worked well in the past century, will most likely have to be changed significantly. Being prepared for this possibility is critical if the community college is expected to provide the training needed for its students and business community.

Staff will need to be upgraded because of the disruption created by the technology that reaches stage two. Counselors and advisors will need to understand the short-term and long-term directions of the disruptive technology in order to accurately discuss career options for the students. The library staff will need to be upgraded to keep the library holdings and data bases on track with the impact that the technologies will have on teaching and learning. Library holdings may change significantly to more online and internet pathways to information that is continuously kept to state-of-the-art levels.

Step 7: Equipment and Facility Needs

The stage two disruptions may very well create the need for new equipment beyond what the college currently holds. The question may be whether to purchase or lease the equipment, a decision that will have to be made when the equipment needs are determined. Corequisite with equipment may come the need for renovating existing buildings or constructing entirely new facilities. Determining what has to be done will take preparation before stage two arrives, followed with rapid actions when the needs are known.

Step 8: Research Committee

If the committees researching the technologies and their movement toward stage two are thorough and accurate, their reporting will make the decision making for each technology more reasonable and obtainable. This kind of work at the community college level will become extremely important to the successful development of the college to stay abreast of what is happening, what changes are obvious, what retraining is needed, and what equipment and facilities must be procured. The time, efforts, and costs of research will pay off when it is done continuously, accurately, and thoroughly. Research will become a bedrock of the successful community college.

Step 9: Success and Viability

Keeping the community college viable in the twenty-first century will take a different kind of mindset than that needed previously. "Creating a vision, translating it into a future-back strategy, and then programming and implementing is not a discrete event within a corporation's life. In a way, it *is* its life" (Johnson et al., 2020, p. 138). The research committees will assist the college leadership greatly in understanding the coming disruptions, when to deal with them, and how to use them to the greatest advantage. That approach is rapidly becoming the pathway of business leaders. Educational leaders cannot not be caught with ignorance.

GROWTH MINDSET

Carol Dweck (2006) in her book, *Mindset: The New Psychology of Success: How We can Learn to Fulfill Our Potential*, envisioned what would be needed for success on the individual and corporate level when she discussed the need for a growth mindset. "People with a growth mindset are constantly monitoring what's going on. . ." (Dweck, 2006, p. 215). Her idea was a harbinger of what was to come. No longer can those in leadership make decisions based on a business-as-usual model. Looking forward always is critical. Jeff Bezos, the successful leader of Amazon, took a similar view, "Focus on the long term. It's all about the long term (Bezos, 2021, p. 21).

FINDINGS

Although there are many researchers who study leadership in the current century and others who lead successfully in it, there is not time or space in this book to provide information from all of them. One more is worthwhile though, "Google hasn't kept pace by milking a single product. It's repeatedly reinvented itself—and search, in specific—to keep up with changing consumer preferences, and its success can be traced to its ability to do so" (Kantrowitz, (2020), p. 95). Always looking ahead, always searching, is the mantra of the successful business in the current century. The business community provides a model for community college leaders to learn, follow, and adapt to their needs in order to create a successful and viable institution.

CONCLUSION

The pathway into the successful future of the community college will rely on leadership that is aware of what is on the horizon, researching the development of the findings, making plans to deal with future issues, and taking action to keep the community college movement alive, vibrant, and successful in the mid-twenty-first century. As time moves the world through the remaining middle of the century, those in leadership positions will need a solid foundation to work from, one that those in leadership positions today can creatively construct. The pathway will literally be built as the years go by. It will take wisdom, creativity, and inventiveness based in solid research to successfully use future-back planning for the benefit of all concerned.

CHAPTER 10 SUMMARY

- With ten technologies, including three potential game-changers, already in existence with more to come, presidential leadership in the community college sector is facing potential disruptions to business as usual in the near future.

- A two-phase system can be used to help guide the community college president through the potentially difficult issues the institution may face.

Phase 1:

- *Step 1: Determination*: At each community college, determine which of the ten technologies will have the potential to impact the college.
- Some of the ten, such as artificial intelligence and quantum computing, will have an effect on the operation of the college no matter the size or location of the college; the question is when and to what degree?
- *Step 2: Initial Internal Communication*: Once a college has determined which of the technologies will most likely affect the college, that list should be communicated throughout the institution to administrators, faculty, staff, students, and board members.
- *Step 3: Research Committees*: Appropriate internal committees should be developed to study the individual technologies understood to have the potential to disrupt specific areas of the college.
- *Step 4: External Communication*: Once the college has set the various committees into operation, it is important to inform the external stakeholders of what the college is doing and how it will benefit external stakeholders in the business community and potential students.
- Students will be very interested to know that the college is investigating what the future business, health, and technical fields will hold for them.
- *Step 5: Periodic Internal Communication*: Since the various committees are studying and researching information about a specific technology, it is important to have each committee make periodic reports.
- Transparency is very important as there are some technologies that may cause serious disruptions that will affect many or all of the faculty and staff.
- Careful research, periodic updating, and caring for all faculty and staff is critically important when a technology reaches stage two and impacts the institution.

Phase 2:

- *Step 6: Retraining of Faculty and Staff:* Since the development of the ten technologies will at some point reach stage two, with associated disruptions within the institution that directly affect some faculty and staff, the college must be prepared financially to support any retraining or reeducation needed to meet the needs required.
- Faculty will need to be developed for meeting the needs for changes in existing courses, preparing new courses and in many cases, and developing an entirely new program at the certificate or associate degree level.
- Staff too will need to be upgraded because of the disruption created by the technology that reaches stage two.
- *Step 7: Equipment and Facility Needs:* The stage two disruptions may very well create the need for new equipment beyond what the college currently holds.
- Determining what has to be done will take preparation before stage 2 arrives, with rapid actions when the needs are known.
- *Step 8: Research Committees:* If the committees researching the technologies and their movement toward stage two are thorough and accurate, their reporting will make the decision making for each technology more reasonable and obtainable.
- The time, efforts, and costs of research will pay off when it is done continuously, accurately, and thoroughly.
- Research will become a bedrock of the successful community college.
- *Step 9: Success and Viability:* Keeping the community college viable in the twenty-first century will take a different kind of mindset than that needed previously.
- Always looking ahead, always searching, is the mantra of the successful business in the current century.
- The business community provides a model for community college leaders to learn, follow, and adapt to their needs in order to create a successful and viable institution.
- As time moves the world through the remaining half of the century, those in leadership positions will need a solid foundation to work

from, one that those in leadership positions today can creatively construct.

Chapter 11

Commingling with Business

Up to this point, the book has focused for the most part on the directions and actions the community college leader can take internally. However, there are other alternatives, one of which has been in existence already in the late twentieth century in some European countries. That method is to integrate the business with the educational institution to the point where the educational institution resides within the business. It takes a rather large business to accomplish this possibility, but it already exists to some degree in Europe. It most likely started with an apprenticeship program, which are historically prevalent in those countries.

SYMBIOTIC RELATIONSHIPS

Apprenticeship programs have been growing almost exponentially in the United States during the past two decades. They establish close, almost symbiotic relationships between the business and the community college. The business provides the environment for hands-on experience and the college provides the academic instruction. Over time, the business and the educational institution work so well together that for the benefit of the student it would be a small step to commingle the two.

EXAMPLES

That kind of closer relationship developed between a medical center and a community college in Virginia. The medical center taught the hands-on portion of the curriculum, and the community college taught the academic courses in science, math, psychology, English and the like. The entire program, a three-year experience for the student, worked very well for the medical center, the community college, the students, and the community in general. It is a good example of comingling the business and the educational institution.

Another one almost developed between that community college and a nuclear maintenance business. The nuclear maintenance business wanted to expand into nuclear power plant construction and needed about three hundred additional engineers. When the company tried to hire that many engineers within a matter of a very few years, it knew it was in trouble. The managers decided that they wanted local individuals, who after obtaining their B.S. in engineering degrees, would hopefully remain with the company longer that those hired from the outside the area.

The company was willing to pay the tuition, books, and fees for the students while they attended college, and the company hired the students while they were taking courses to work part-time and pay them as employees. When the students obtained their degree in engineering, they were offered a position at the company.

The company leadership also knew it would take a university to work with the community college in order for students to obtain the B.S. degree in engineering. In addition, the company wanted the university to teach its courses at the community college location to allow the students to live at home if they wished. The business leaders were willing to offer the university a considerable sum of funding to initiate such a program. Long story short, the community college, a university, and the company worked out an agreement to offer this program. Students were enrolled at the community college and began the educational journey to an engineering degree at no cost to them and a certain job at the end of their educational experience.

Over time, that particular program did not succeed as the business had to change its direction and did not pursue the plan to construct nuclear power plants. However, it does demonstrate how the needs to serve a business through the educational development of students' skills and abilities could work for the benefit of all concerned. This could be a good model for community college/university/business education in the future. Programs similar as described above do already exist between some community colleges and businesses. In the future, this model could become more developed and assist both educational institutions and businesses.

MEETING THE WORKFORCE NEEDS IN THE TWENTY-FIRST CENTURY

Community colleges could partner with a large business or a set of businesses to meet the workforce needs with the company(s) underwriting the tuition, fees, and books of the students and hiring the students part-time to work in the business while they are pursuing their education. This could be a very easy step by taking what are now apprenticeships and internships into a program that would be integrated into the businesses. It could be of great benefit to the student, the community college, the business involved, and the local community.

Students would obtain a certificate or associate's degree at no expense, the businesses would receive entry level workforce individuals working for them part-time, and the community college would enroll students who mostly likely would be retained until graduation. Students could gain experience in an actual business environment and decide whether they liked it or not. Businesses could get a good look at the student's work habits, skills, and abilities while being part-time employed within the business. The college could update its program as required to keep up with the training needs of the business.

ASSISTANCE FROM THE BUSINESS COMMUNITY

In addition, the business could assist the community college in obtaining state-of-the-art equipment for the training at considerably less cost than normal. It could provide donations to the college to support the program and it could allow students of learn on equipment at the business location itself. The fact that the students graduated with experience in the business and the kind of equipment used in the facility would benefit both the student and the business. The community college would gain student numbers and a close working relationship with the business, which in the long run could generate donations from the business in fund-raising campaigns.

CONCLUSION

The advantages of the community college comingling with local businesses are beneficial for all concerned. In the long run, the close working relationship between the community college and the businesses would create a very stable economic situation for all concerned. Integrating education and training with business needs is a rather small step for the community college as well as the business community. It will take leaders at the college and leaders at the businesses to see the benefits of such a process and work together to make it a reality. It is a very doable method for any community college large or small.

CHAPTER 11 SUMMARY

- Up to this point, the book has focused for the most part on the directions and actions the community college leader can take internally within the institution with input from the external business world.
- However, there are other alternatives, one of which has been in existence already in the late twentieth century in some European countries.
- Apprenticeship programs have been growing almost exponentially in the United States during the past two decades.
- Over time, the business and the educational institution work so well together for the benefit of the student that it is just a small step to commingle the two.
- That kind of closer relationship developed between a medical center and a community college in Virginia.
- Another one almost developed between that community college and a nuclear maintenance business.
- In the future, this model could become more developed and assist both educational institutions and businesses.
- Community colleges could partner with a large business or a set of businesses to meet the workforce needs with the company(s) underwriting the tuition, fees, and books of the student and hire the student part-time to work in the business.

- Students would obtain a certificate or associate's degree at no expense, the businesses would receive entry workforce individuals working for them part-time, and the community college would enroll students who mostly likely would be retained until graduation.
- In the long run, the close working relationship between the community college and businesses would create a very stable economic situation for all concerned.

Chapter 12

Eye to the Future

The twenty-first century must be understood as different from preceding century in terms of the ten technologies and others that are developing and will reach the exponential stage in the foreseeable number of years. The ten technologies are not science fiction; they are not just grand creative schemes. They are, for lack of a better term, science-fact. They will require community college leaders who are continuously future-focused and thrive on change and disruption. The business world already is beginning to understand that this kind of leader will be needed in the successful business of the twenty-first century. What can be learned to develop successful leaders in the community college world?

ALWAYS DAY ONE

Successful business leaders in this century will operate as if it is "always day one," an entrepreneurial approach to business (Kantrowitz, 2020). It will take leaders with a growth mindset. "People in a growth mindset don't just seek challenge, they thrive on it. The bigger the challenge, the more they stretch" (Dweck, 2006, p. 21). When disruptions appear, rather than shy away from them, the successful business leader will figure out how to deal with them and make them integral to the business. However, we must not forget that ". . .the pace of change is not simply faster—it's accelerating and that's a completely different story" (Gutsche, 2020, p. 88).

Leading from the Future

Further, it is critical to lead from the future. Leaders must research what is coming, develop a future-back vision, and create a plan for success in the future (Johnson et al., 2020). According to the highly successful CEO of Amazon, Jeff Bezos, "Long term thinking levers our existing abilities and lets us do new things we couldn't otherwise contemplate" (Bezos, 2021, p. 84). Those in business and those researching business in the twenty-first century agree that the changes coming because of the disruptions caused by technologies will cause significant modifications in the way successful business leaders will operate.

Although community college leaders may only begin to become aware that twentieth century models for leadership are not working as well as expected, they, like their counterparts in the business community, must learn rapidly what they will be required do to be successful as educational leaders in the coming years. This is not a time to sit back and take a wait and see approach. Rather, this is a time to become educated on what the disruptions of currently ten technologies will have on community college through vigorous research. From there, they will have to do serious preparation for what is to come.

ADVICE ON PLANNING

The following advice is offered to planners to cope with unexpected events:

- Begin by admitting that no forecast or plan is ever complete.
- Use expert imagination to identify potential changes and black swans.
- Monitor real time data to see whether there are emerging changes to forecasts and plans
- Think in terms of multiple possible future conditions (scenarios) and multiple variations in plans to cover any number of contingencies.
- Learn to be more flexible and willing to adapt when circumstances are known to justify changes in forecasts and plans (Millett, 2011, p. 111).

It will be critical to assume a growth mindset, operate as if it is always day one, think long term, and plan from the future-back. Those who are able to do so, have the best chance of leading successful community colleges into the future for the benefit of students, the college, faculty, staff, the business community, and local economic development. If business leaders can keep their businesses on an even keel in disruptive waters, community college leaders can do the same as well. The community college mission is too important to do otherwise.

ONE MORE THING

One more thing, funding for two-year colleges has over the decades been a real problem. In the very beginning junior colleges were funded by universities. The funding soon spread to communities where the independent junior colleges were located. Some states early on decided to fund the two-year colleges with state funding, others, a combination of state and local funding. Of course, student tuition always provided some portion of the costs, but never enough for the institution to survive.

GOING BEYOND

Already in the latter twentieth century, a few community colleges went beyond those funding sources. This entails developing a revenue stream separate from the usual state funding, local funding and student tuition. One university found that because of its location close to the ocean and a tourist destination that it could attract numerous out-of-state students. This was advantageous because the out-of-state tuition per student was close to what the university would obtain per student from the state, local, and student funding. As a result, the institution increased its marketing to out-of-state students significantly to the point where its leaders rarely requested additional funding from the state and local sources.

A community college constructed a hotel facility that was used for hospitality training for the students and a revenue stream for the college. Another institution incorporated veterinary programs with horse training programs and horse shows, which again provided student training and a funding source for the college. A third created a standalone manufacturing technology institute that served the business community with the latest in technological advances. It brought in the latest in machine tool, and 3D printing equipment which could be used for the creation of prototypes for the business community. This work with the business community provided an additional revenue stream for the college.

Since most community colleges currently have a foundation that can raise funds for the institution, it could buy a franchise in a business with the proceeds going to underwrite the college budget. This may seem like an unusual way to create a revenue stream for the institution, but in the twenty-first century it will make sense and has the potential to become common practice. In other words, rather than operate the community college solely with the usual state, local, and student tuition funding, the college could ensure its ability to continue to serve the needs of students, the business community, and local economic development by using methods that make sense in the rapidly changing, disruptive environment of the twenty-first century.

At the moment, these examples are used by a very few community colleges; however, they could be the harbinger of a direction community colleges could take in the future. Using the college foundations, community colleges could develop alternative funding sources that could be depended on from year to year. It will take imagination and an entrepreneurial spirit on the part of the college leadership.

CONCLUSION

The community college in the twenty-first century will need to develop into a teaching/learning center of the kind not seen as yet. It will serve students, the business community, local economic development, and the community in general in ways only dreamed of in the past or not as yet even thought of. It will be critical that all community college leaders be hired with entrepreneurial experience, imaginative thinking, at ease with transparency, ability to see though disruptions, and excellent communication skills internally and externally, combined with a caring personality.

CHAPTER 12 SUMMARY

- The twenty-first century must be understood as different from preceding centuries in terms of the ten technologies and others that are developing and will reach the exponential stage in the foreseeable number of years.
- The business world is already beginning to understand that this kind of leader will be needed in the successful business of the twenty-first century.
- When the disruptions appear, rather than shy away from them, the successful business leader will figure out how to deal with them and make them integral to the business.
- Those in business and those researching business in the twenty-first century agree that the changes coming because of the disruptions caused by technologies will cause a significant modification in the way successful business leaders will operate.
- This is a time to become educated on what the disruptions of currently ten technologies will have on community college through vigorous research.
- Rather, this is a time to become educated on what the disruptions of currently ten technologies will have on community college through vigorous research.
- It will be critical to assume a growth mindset, operate as if it is always day one, think long term, and plan from the future-back.
- Already in the late twentieth century, a few community colleges went beyond those funding sources.
- Since most community colleges currently have a foundation that can raise funds for the institution, it could buy a franchise in a business with the proceeds going to underwrite the college budget.
- At the moment, these examples are used by a very few community colleges; however, they could also be the harbinger of a direction community colleges could take in the future.
- It will be critical that all community college leaders be hired with entrepreneurial experience, imaginative thinking, at ease with transparency, ability to see though disruptions, and excellent communication skills internally and externally, combined with a caring personality.

Epilogue

The idea for this book came from research into the ten technologies, the impact they will have on the business community, and the search for sources that provide support and guidance for community college leaders in the twenty-first century. Already there exists a canon of books that provide guidance, models, and methods to the business CEO. There are also books discussing twenty-first century leadership in regard to the disruptions of technologies at the public school level. However, there is a dearth of books on the topic for community college administrators. Consequently, the changes needed in community college leadership, and the development of the technologies of the current century, led to the development of this book.

This is a beginning look at the technologies that will face the community college administrator in the twenty-first century. combined with some ideas as to how to deal with the disruptions they will bring. Hopefully this book will help those in community college leadership to have a place to begin their considerations of what to do in a stage 2, the exponentially disruptive environment that the ten technologies will bring. Perhaps it will encourage others to research and write their findings and concepts that will help to keep community colleges successful and viable in the twenty-first century.

Appendix
Guiding the Community College: A Two-Phase System

Phase 1: Preparation

Step 1: Determining: At each community college, it will be necessary to begin by determining which of the ten technologies will have the potential to impact the college.

Step 2: Initial Internal Communication: Once a college has determined which of the technologies will most likely affect the college, that list should be communicated throughout the institution to administrators, faculty, staff, students, and board members.

Step 3: Research Committees: Appropriate internal committees should be developed to study the individual technologies understood to have the potential to disrupt a specific area of the college, such as the automotive department or in the case of IoT, the business department.

Step 4: External Communication: Once the college has set the various committees into operation, it is important to inform the external stakeholders of what the college is doing and how it will benefit those in the business community, and potential students.

Step 5: Periodic Internal Communication: Since the various committees are studying and researching information about a specific technology, it is important to have each committee make periodic reports.

Phase 2: Implementation

Step 6: Retraining of Faculty and Staff: Since the development of the ten technologies will at some point reach stage 2, with associated disruptions within the institution that directly affect some faculty and staff, the college must be prepared financially to support any retraining or reeducation needed to meet the needs required.

Step 7: Equipment and Facility Needs: The stage two disruptions may very well create the need for new equipment beyond what the college currently holds.

Step 8: Research Committees: If the committees researching the technologies and their movement toward stage two are thorough and accurate, their reporting will make the decision making for each technology more reasonable and obtainable.

Step 9: Success and Viability: Keeping the community college viable in the twenty-first century will take a different kind of mindset than that needed previously.

References

Ace, X. *The history of youtube.* Retrieved from https://wwwengadget.com
Ark, T.V., & Wise B. (2011). Getting Smart: How digital learning is changing the world. Retrieved from https://search-proquest-com.proxy 200.nclive.org/central/docview/2130990897/bookReader?accountid=15065.
Aspen Institute & Achieving the Dream. (2013). *Crisis and Opportunity: Aligning the community college presidency with student success.* Retrieved from https://files.eric.ed.gov/fulltext/ED553654.pdf
Bailenson, J. (2018). Experience on Demand: *What virtual reality is, how it works, and what it can do.* New York: W.W. Norton & Company.
Bailey, T., Jaggers, S., & Jenkins, D. (2015). *Redesigning America's community colleges.* Cambridge, MA: Harvard University Press.
Bell, S. (2010). Project based learning for the twenty-first century: Skills for the future. *The Clearing House: A journal of educational strategies, issues and ideas*, 83. doi:10.1080/00098650903505415.
Bergman, J., & Sams, A. (2012). *Flip your classroom: Reach every student in every class every day.* Eugene, OR: International Society for Technology in Education.
Bezos, J. (2021). *Invent and wander: The collected writings of Jeff Bezos.* Cambridge, MA: Harvard Business Review Press.
Doudna, J., & Sternberg, S. (2017). *A crack in creation: Gene editing and the unthinkable power to control evolution.* Boston: Houghton Mifflin Harcourt.
Dweck, C. (2006). *Mindset the new psychology of success: How we can learn to fulfill our potential.* New York: Ballantine Books.
Fisher, J. (1984). *Power of the Presidency.* London: Macmillan Publishing.
Fuller, R.B. (1969). *Operating manual for spaceship earth.* New York: Simon & Schuster.

Gutsche, J. (2020). *Create the future: Tactics for disruptive thinking.* New York: Fast Company Press.

Johnson, M., & Suskewicz, J. (2020). *Lead from the future: How to turn visionary thinking into breakthrough growth.* Cambridge, MA: Harvard Business Review Press.

Kane, J., Phillips, A., Copulsky, J., & Andrus, G. (2019). *The technology fallacy: How people are the real key to digital transformation.* Cambridge, MA: The MIT Press.

Kantrowitz, A. (2020*). Always day one: How the tech titans plan to stay on top forever.* New York: Penguin.

Kurzweil, R. (2005). *The Singularity is Near.* New York: Penguin.

Merisotis, J. (2020). *Human work in the age of machines.* New York: Rosetta Books.

Millett, S. (2011). *Managing the future: A guide to forecasting and strategic planning in the 21st century.* Charmouth, UK: Triarchy Press.

Morrison, E., Hutcheson, S., Nilsen, E., Fadden, J., & Franklin, N. (2019). *Strategic doing: Ten skills for agile leadership.* Hoboken, NJ: Wiley.

Sahlins, M., & Service E. (1960). *Evolution and culture.* Ann Arbor: University of Michigan Press.

Schwab, K. (2018). *Shaping the fourth industrial revolution.* Cologny, Switzerland: World Economic Forum.

Staat, D. (2020). *Student-Focused learning, Higher Education in an Exponential Digital Era.* Lanham, MD: Rowman & Littlefield.

Vaughan, G., & Associates. (1983). *Issues for community college leaders in a new era.* Hoboken, NJ: Jossey-Bass.

Wiggins, B. (2016). An overview and study on the use of games, simulations, and gamification in higher education. *International Journal of Game-Based Learning,* 6, 18–28. https://doi.org/10.4018/IJGBL.2016010102.

Willyerd, K., & Mistick, B. (2016). *Stretch: How to future-proof yourself for tomorrow's workplace.* Hoboken, NJ: Wiley.

About the Author

Darrel W. Staat received his doctorate from the University of Michigan, master's degree from Western Michigan University, and bachelor's degree from Hope College in Holland, Michigan. Over the years, he has taught a series of undergraduate and graduate courses.

He currently holds the position of coordinator and associate professor in the Higher Education Executive Leadership program at Wingate University in Wingate, North Carolina. Previously he held the position of president of the South Carolina Technical College System in Columbia, South Carolina; president of Central Virginia Community College in Lynchburg, Virginia; the founding president of York County Community College in Wells, Maine; and president of Eastern Maine Community College in Bangor, Maine. Dr. Staat's previous book publications include:

- *Virtual Reality in Higher Education: Instruction for the Digital Age* (2021)
- *Higher Education Planning in an Exponential Age: A Continuous, Dynamic Process* (2021)
- *Student-Focused Learning: Higher Education in an Exponential Digital Era* (2020)
- *A Baseline of Development: Higher Education and Technology* (2019)

- *Exponential Technologies: Higher Education in an Era of Serial Disruptions* (2019)
- *Facing an Exponential Future: Technology and the Community College* (2018)

www.ingramcontent.com/pod-product-compliance
Lightning Source LLC
Chambersburg PA
CBHW020126240426
43673CB00038B/606